LEADERSHIP IN ACTION:

INSPIRING STORIES AND STRATEGIES FOR GROWTH

REAL-LIFE CASE STUDIES, PRACTICAL ADVICE, AND PATHWAYS TO SUCCESS

PADMA C

Clever Fox® PUBLISHING

Chennai • Bangalore

CLEVER FOX PUBLISHING
Chennai, India

Published by CLEVER FOX PUBLISHING 2025

ISBN: 978-93-6707-253-0

FOREWORD

Business leadership is many dimensional and contextual. Definition of success of both the leader and the organisation vary. Leader is more than a manager, path to leadership isn't just paved with competence and credentials, but with resilience, visibility, self-belief, and an ability to understand and act on complexity and uncertainty without compromising on core values. *Leadership in Action* offers a lens into such leaders their contexts and measures of success.

What makes this book powerful is its truth-telling. It doesn't offer platitudes or one-size-fits-all formulas. These pages aren't filled with hypotheticals—they pulse with lived experiences. Through the Voices of individuals across industries, we uncover what leadership really looks like: confronting bias, managing complex trade-offs, and staying resilient in the face of doubt. Each story is a lesson.

Good books on leadership are not prescriptive. They should give an opportunity for the reader to empathise, relate and learn from such experiences. Padma's voice throughout is that of a guide—discreet yet analytical, reflective yet grounded. She curates experiences with care, distils insights with clarity, and invites readers to claim space in their own journeys. With empathy and structure, she transforms hard-won lessons into frameworks that are easy to understand —not just with strategy, but with purpose. It is an invitation—to reflect deeply, to act deliberately, and to lead authentically. For those ready to unlearn, to listen, and to evolve—this should give great insights.

For every mid-career professional seeking renewed agency; and for every ambitious early-career individual looking for a compass before the crossroads—this book is relevant.

In a time when authentic leadership is more needed than ever, *Leadership in Action* is a timely, generous companion.

Mr. Srikar Reddy P.
Exec Vice Chairman, Sonata Software

ACKNOWLEDGMENTS

This book is a result of shared experiences of my friends and acquaintances. I felt a strong need for such a book to guide individuals in their career progression.

A big thanks for all the contributors who came out with honesty, courage, and grace in sharing their stories. Each one is highly meritorious and have conveyed very valuable lessons of life and career, by sharing their own stories with intensity and clarity. You all voice the different dimensions of leadership and achievement.

To my mentors, peers, and friends across HAL, Sonata Software, and Altumind—you have given me the confidence and courage to bring forth this book. The learnings and guidance from each one of you are invaluable and I attempted to convey some of those through this book.

A special note of gratitude to Inspiring Jatin. But for his coaching and push, I would not have started this book. Your guidance during the "Best Selling Author Mastery Program" made me reinvent myself into the new dimension and bring forth my long pending ambition of becoming an author.

To my parents, who have been my pillars of support all through with unending confidence in me. To my dear family—thank you for being my grounding force and my greatest cheerleaders. This journey would not have unfolded the same without your love and patience.

To every woman who has ever questioned her place at the table, or reimagined her worth outside the margins—you were always the true inspiration. This book is dedicated to you.

Lastly, to those readers who carry ambition quietly and lead with both soul and structure—may this book serve as a companion in your climb.

ABOUT THE AUTHOR

Padma is a Senior Delivery Architect and Governance Specialist with over 30 years of leadership experience across Aerospace, Information Technology, and the Public Sector. An alumna of ***NIT Warangal*** and ***IIT Kharagpur***, she began her career at ***HAL,*** moving to lead global programs and tech transformation at ***Sonata Software;*** and then serving as ***COO at Altumind.*** Certified as an Independent Director (IICA), Padma specializes in process excellence, talent development strategies, and effective organization building. ***Leadership in Action*** reflects her bold vision: to empower leaders to create ecosystems for the progress and development of all.

ABOUT THE CONTRIBUTORS

Nemichandra: *The first lady Chief Designer and second lady General Manager of HAL, who played a crucial role in Mission Systems and Weapon Systems Integration on indigenously designed helicopters. She is also a well-known author in Kannada.*

Ravi C: *His inspiring journey from India to Germany and Norway illustrates the transition from engineering to becoming a sought-after SAP consultant, showcasing leadership in managing international programs.*

Sonali Dutta: *Independent Director, Former VP of Corporate Affairs & HR, Bry-Air. Organic Farmer, Advisor & Mentor, National President-Corporate Sustainability Council, WICCI. Committed to guiding organizations and individuals towards responsible growth.*

Srinivasa Prasad: *VP/Technical Director in the edible oil industry.*

Smita Priyadarshini: *Acclaimed lawyer and Senior Director at BCG – is a pioneering force at the intersection of law and leadership. With a distinguished career and unwavering advocacy, she has inspired and empowered a generation of women lawyers to lead with purpose and confidence.*

Nayeema Kouser, *ICWAI, IIMB: Center Head at Sinch Cloud Communications, she champions the setup of GCCs and drives their success.*

Abha Saxena: *the Founder and CEO of Social Equity Advisory Services.*

Dr. Ambuja Udas: *From STEM stream, a well-accomplished scientist at BARC*

Dr. Gayatri Aditya: *Principal at Sir MVSA, researcher, architect, planner, educator, and entrepreneur, she inspires hundreds of young architects.*

Meera K.S.: *Veteran IT professional*

Dr. Subhadra Jalali: *One amongst the first female retinal surgeons in India, she has made pioneering advancements in newborn eye care that have positively impacted thousands worldwide.*

Sunil Khurana: *Executive Chairman of BPL Medical Technologies.*

TABLE OF CONTENTS

CHAPTER 1

INTRODUCTION

There is plenty of advice available for those looking to advance their careers. From Stephen Covey's timeless *The 7 Habits of Highly Effective People* to countless modern leadership and professional development manuals, the fundamentals are extensively covered. But here's the truth: mastering the fundamentals—such as strategic thinking, integrity, and continual learning—is only half the struggle. What about the subtle, frequently unnoticed obstacles that can hold back even the most competent professionals?

This book is about those hidden obstacles. It's about the "fine print" of career advancement—the stuff that no one talks about but everyone experiences. Whether it's developing a personal brand, navigating workplace power-play, or learning to advocate for yourself without seeming arrogant, these are the skills that separate those who plateau from those who soar.

Let me share a story:

It was appraisal day. Suhasini (name changed) woke up in the morning filled with both hope and apprehension. It had been more than six years since her last promotion, and she felt that the last year had been outstanding. All her projects were successful, and she had also played a key role in a significant organizational initiative. She was confident she would advance to a senior management role. She got ready swiftly, hopped into her car, and drove to work.

As the appraisal time approached, her anxiety escalated. With her heart racing, she sat down with her manager for the appraisal discussion. The conversation went smoothly, but her successes were dismissed as simply fulfilling her responsibilities. "In terms of quantitative measures, you're doing well. However, I don't see the qualities needed for promotion." "You excel at work, coordination, leadership, communication, and more, but you aren't enthusiastic enough in some meetings," and so on—seemingly trivial excuses that led to the conclusion that she would not be promoted.

Things had been quite different before her last promotion to the highest middle manager level. She was one of the fastest advancing professionals, and everyone expected her to reach the upper echelons swiftly. Heartbroken and disheartened, Suhasini returned home feeling heavy-hearted. After a few days of silent resistance and tension with her immediate manager, things gradually returned to normal.

Then she started working on advocating her work – speaking about her achievements in different meetings, coming forward to take on complex and critical projects, and participating actively in the meetings. This gained the attention of the decision makers. With this, she got the required recognition in terms of promotion and hike. This is a perfect example of how mastering the usually ignored aspects will make a big difference.

Another story of Vidyarthi (name changed):

Vidyarthi attended an interview for the top position and was waiting for the results. He received a regret letter. This happened for four consecutive years. Each time, some or the other bias, such as regional bias or caste bias, came into the picture. Then he understood the importance of negotiation and assertiveness. With persistent efforts of being assertive and negotiating, he achieved the goals that he set for himself.

Career Stagnation in Middle Management

Reaching the highest levels of management is a highly sought-after objective for many professionals at mid- and senior levels.

However, most middle managers experience career stagnation and get stuck at mid-level for extended periods. Consistent performance evaluations may include phrases like:

- "You still have room for improvement."
- "You need to adopt a more strategic mindset."
- "You are overly empathetic and lack the necessary detachment."

With such persistent critiques, individuals may lose self-confidence and develop self-doubt. Below are some reasons for this behavior among managers:

1. Systemic Barriers

Office Power-play: Organizations can form power centers where different groups compete, often leading to suppression of less powerful groups. One must be sensitive to these political aspects and tread carefully.

Invisible Hurdles: Perceptions and biases—shaped by style, age, gender, and experience—create obstacles to advancement. Some biases are conscious, while others are unconscious. The term "Glass Ceiling," introduced by Marilyn Loden in 1978, describes barriers that prevent women and minorities from reaching elite roles despite their qualifications. Key statistics highlighting systemic obstacles for women in the corporate environment can be found in the Appendix of this book.

Favoritism: Many individual case studies illustrate how these issues manifest and how different people have overcome them.

2. Lack of Networking & Mentoring

At junior levels, many individuals focus solely on their work, which is appropriate for that level. But as the level increases, Mid-management levels also, people don't change their behaviour, believing, "My work should speak for itself." While direct supervisors may recognize their efforts, higher management often remains unaware. Gaining visibility in a positive way and participating in broader organizational issues beyond one's project is crucial. Additionally, mentoring—both seeking guidance and mentoring others—is often neglected. Many individuals lose direction and feel stuck; mentoring can help navigate these challenges.

3. Difficulty in Negotiating Promotions, hikes

Many individuals think, "I don't want to beg for my promotion or hike," or "My manager knows my worth." However, when promotion time comes, they may hesitate to ask for what they deserve.

4. Pressures on Work-Life Balance

The demand for higher performance can lead to neglecting work-life balance, resulting in burnout that adversely affects personal health and job effectiveness.

5. Lack of Self-Awareness and Empowerment

As individuals climb the corporate ladder, available positions decrease, leading to intense competition among equally qualified colleagues. Key challenges include:

Skill Deficiency: Top management roles require a wider range of skills, including technological proficiency, negotiation, strategic thinking, stakeholder engagement, and emotional intelligence. These may not have been fully cultivated in earlier positions.

Adaptability: The fast pace of technological and organizational transformations necessitates continual upskilling. A lack of self-understanding, personality development training, and knowledge of individual strengths can lead to stress and demotivation.

These factors contribute to career stagnation, where individuals often face no promotions and experience pay disparity compared to peers, leading to feelings of depression and demotivation. This can also trigger impostor syndrome.

Organizations suffer as well; sidelining deserving candidates can demotivate not only the individual but also others in the workplace.

It's crucial to resist being adversely affected by outside negativity that could compromise one's professional achievements.

Purpose of This Book

This book is for anyone who has ever felt trapped, overlooked, or unsure about how to move forward in their career. It's not enough to know what you need to do; you also need to know how to execute it authentically and sustainably. Let's go beyond the basics and tackle the real, often unspoken challenges of career advancement together.

This book isn't just about theory; it's about action. We'll address genuine problems in job advancement: overcoming impostor syndrome, navigating office power-play, building a personal brand, and finding the courage to pursue work that aligns with your values.

What to Expect

- **Anecdotes and Insights**: Learn from those who have been where you are and emerged stronger.
- **Theory and Practical Exercises**: Implement strategies for each aspect discussed.

- **Career Advancement Strategies**: Summaries from various case studies.
- **Extra Tips**: Specific guidance for women and minorities aiming to break the glass ceiling.

Whether you're just starting out, hitting a mid-career slump, or contemplating a complete reinvention, this book will meet you where you are. We will move beyond surface-level advice and confront the real challenges of career growth together.

Final Thoughts

Career advancement requires more than just hard work and successful outcomes. It's also about relationships, visibility, and resilience. It's about knowing when to negotiate, how to network effectively, and having mature mentors. Striking a balance between ambition and authenticity, as well as work and life, is essential. These are the issues that most career manuals skip over, but they can make or break your career.

In the following chapters, each of these issues are dealt with in detail. Real-life journeys of individuals from diverse fields—engineering, IT, oil & gas, agriculture, medical devices, academia, finance, law, medicine, and more—who have overcome personal, professional, and societal challenges to become leaders are presented in each chapter. These stories highlight the core elements of leadership: resilience, adaptability, self-belief, and the courage to challenge limits. While the stories are real, some names have been changed to protect privacy.

CHAPTER 2

OVERCOMING SYSTEMIC BARRIERS - HOW TO NAVIGATE BIASES, OFFICE POWER-PLAY, AND OTHER INVISIBLE HURDLES

In a time when, where things change quickly, it's important to get past structural barriers and question deeply held beliefs to encourage innovation, inclusion, and personal growth. These problems are usually caused by how an organization works, old habits, and deeply held beliefs that get in the way of growth and creativity. To overcome these problems, you must first understand where they come from and how they affect the way work gets done, then develop ways to get around and overcome them.

All the leaders in this book expressed the systemic obstacles they faced in their professional and personal journeys. A select few are presented in this section, where this aspect is demonstrated more dominantly than others.

"Designing with precision, leading with vision." Nemichandra

(PG in 1985; Retd. Chief Designer & General Manager, HAL)

"Do not be intimidated by circumstances; believe in your strength."

"Know your job well; that gives immense confidence."

"Do not hesitate to point out discriminatory acts."

"Our generation of women engineers worked with a historical responsibility on their shoulders."

"We have come a long way from the 'It's Barbie dolls for girls and Airplanes for boys' era."

Breaking Barriers in Aerospace: A Journey of Courage and Innovation

Here is the story of a woman with diverse achievements, from integrating weapon systems on helicopters to traveling across the world, a being board member of a software company, and still finding time to work for social causes. She remained steadfast on the mission of gender equality; while becoming a well-known author and, motivational speaker. Here is her story.

'Women cannot be taken onboard a warship'; she had a unique problem in March 1998 when she arrived in Mumbai as the only woman on a team tasked with integrating the advanced torpedo system on a Chetak MATCH role helicopter. The torpedo is an electronically intensive weapon that is used against a Submarine. Just now, as she was embarking the warship, the men standing in a row had smartly saluted her. Taken aback when she had asked, she was told, 'because we thought you were the wife of some senior officer who has come to see the warship.' As she introduced herself as the engineer from Hindustan Aeronautics Limited, who was there for the 'torpedo trials' that required her to sail on the warship, she was told that women could not be taken onboard the warship. Incidentally, she was unaware of the Indian Navy's custom of saluting all women when they embark on a ship as a mark of respect.

She was responsible for the 'weapon release and safety circuits' and integration of the 'torpedo electronic unit' on the helicopter. The flight trials were to take place somewhere deep in the Arabian Sea. As the only design engineer involved in modifying the onboard circuits to suit the present integration, she was required to be onboard the ship. She was from the Electronics stream and belonged to the Avionics Group of the Helicopter Design Bureau (HDB) of HAL. She already had the requisite clearance from the Naval Headquarters, without which she would not have been there in the first place.

Woman Onboard A Warship

She was told that women cannot be taken onboard a warship as there are no facilities available for women to sail. For this weapon trial, she was to sail the whole day and stay onboard the ship for two nights. The next day, after arriving at the designated area in the Arabian Sea, they were to conduct the torpedo trials. Finally, special permission was arranged for her to sail; to her great relief, she was taken onboard the warship.

She was shown a small cabin with a low-hung ceiling belonging to a senior officer who had vacated it for her stay. A small table fan provided relief in the windowless cabin. There was a narrow bunker-type cot, a small table, a chair, and a steel wash basin with a mirror framed in wood. Next to the mirror was a wooden panel on which red letters read: 'KICK IN FOR EMERGENCY ESCAPE'. She wondered how will she reach that height of about five and a half feet if there is an emergency? Would she be able to kick it hard enough to make it open? Well, the excitement of being on a warship dimmed any such worry.

And, of course, there was no option but to use the toilets meant for men onboard. Whatever the inconveniences, she would not let an opportunity like this go because of her gender. She was also humbled as it opened her eyes to the extreme conditions that our personnel in the Indian Navy work to guard our waters and keep us safe. Space in the warship is at a premium. And on a submarine, it is worse.

As she entered the officer's board room, she was not amused to see this giant poster. The poster had a picture of a ship and read, 'Why is a ship called a 'She'? Oh, there is always a lot of bustle around her and a lot of men. It takes a fortune to keep her looking good. She is absolutely uncontrollable without a man at the helm.' Undoubtedly, it was a man's world. It was a path less traveled or never traveled by women. One of the officers told her, 'You are probably the first lady staying onboard on technical duty.' She was lucky that NHVenkatesh, to whom she reported, never hesitated to send women on any mission. Her work would take her all over India and outside, to the medieval city of Kolomna in Russia, the hottest deserts in Israel, and the coldest firing range in Sweden at the Arctic Circle.

Entering Engineering College

In 1976, when she joined Engineering, it was considered a male domain; only seven girls entered NIE, Mysore, that year. She was once told that it is not the field for women. They said, 'Engineering is challenging; Carpentry, Machine Shop, and Foundry are not for girls.' With much self-doubt, she and her friend entered Engineering College and both of them graduated with university ranks. That is when she realized that nothing is impossible for women. Today in Karnataka, there are Engineering colleges for women!

Childhood – Girls don't require Science!

This reminds her of her childhood. In the 1960s, she did her primary schooling in Tumkur, a small town at that time. In middle school, the girls were taught Home Science, while the boys in her class were taught General Science! During her high school days at Mysore, a prestigious Science Institute conducted a Science Essay Writing competition, and she was one of the few boys and girls who won the prize. They had books as prizes, and of the two books she got, one was about 'Cooking,' and the other was about 'Child-Care'! The boys were given fascinating books on Astronomy, Automobiles, and General Science. If this is what a scientific institute gifted a 13-year-old girl, one could imagine how little encouragement there was for girls to take up Science and Technology.

No Role Model

In all the textbooks she read as a child and teenager, she never saw any mention of women scientists. The little book on Marie Curie, which she was fortunate to find in her father's library, almost described her as an exception.

Decades later, when she actively got involved with literature, Science, engineering, and women's studies, she realized she knew almost nothing about Women Scientists of the past was not because there were so few of them. But the wonderful heritage of women in Science and Technology had never reached us. Women are invisible in History. Her story remained virtually untold and unknown. Hence, women grew up in a sheer vacuum, in an atmosphere that offered no role models for girls taking up Science or Engineering.

Joining HAL in 1985

After her B.E. in Electronics and Communication, she completed her Master's in Engineering through Research from the Indian Institute of Science, Bangalore.

When she joined the Helicopter Design Bureau of HAL in 1985, she was lucky to be part of the Advanced Light Helicopter (ALH) project. ALH is India's first indigenously designed multi-role, multi-mission military helicopter. She was part of the Design Team that saw ALH's journey from the drawing board to the first flight and landing on the highest battlefield in the world!

Journey at HAL

Today, she feels proud that more than 300 ALHs are flying in the Indian Armed Forces.

Her journey at HAL has been fascinating, from Weaponizing Advanced Light Helicopter to Fifth-Generation Fighter Aircraft to Unmanned Aerial Vehicle (UAV)!

As a young Engineer, she was excited enough that she once traveled to Kochi in a midnight passenger train, sitting on a potato sack to ensure that she did not miss the first trial of an indigenously developed Sonar System. Sonar is the sensor used in Antisubmarine Warfare. NPOL (Naval Physical & Oceanographic Laboratory) had developed the indigenous Sonar System. During those days of 'telefax,' communication about the trial had arrived late. Hence, she had to travel by train unreserved.

As the group leader of 'Avionics & Mission Sensors,' deeply involved in Weapon System Integration on ALH, she frequently went on outstation trials.

There were lots of lessons learnt:

(a) Do not be intimidated by circumstances.
(b) Believe in your strength, focus on your abilities.
(c) Know your job well, that gives immense confidence.
(d) Do not hesitate to point out discriminatory acts.

Work-Life Balance

She believes women and organizations work on the principle of reciprocity. She says, 'how much we are ready to give to our company opens up that many learning opportunities. How we balance our work and personal life makes a huge difference'.

She had often missed family functions when she was on outstation duty. She had even missed attending her book release function scheduled on a Sunday, as she was required to be at the office that day for an important presentation to the Raksha Mantri. Her work-life balance was tough, but she could manage.

Historical Responsibility

At Helicopter Design Bureau (HDB), the women engineers never hesitated to travel alone or in a group to any place that their work demanded. They were there in Leh at minus 20 degrees C in 1998 for the first cold weather trials of Advanced Light Helicopter (ALH), when Leh had no regular electricity, and kerosene for the 'Buckara' used for room heating was rationed.

They went everywhere with ALH, as extensive flight trials were required for the indigenously designed helicopter. She says, "Our generation of women engineers worked with a historical responsibility on their shoulders. If we failed, our failure would be generalized as 'women can't do this, women can't go for flight trials, and women can't travel alone.' We knew we were opening the gates of equal opportunities to the next generation of women engineers. Hence, we put in more than our best effort."

We held important portfolios

We could consider the women engineers who joined HAL, NAL, and DRDO between 1965 and 1990 as the first-generation women in the aeronautical field.

Nemichandra always felt blessed to be working at HAL, where they were empowered with unique opportunities in their chosen field of specialization. HAL provided them with the best working environment. The women at Helicopter R&D Centre held important portfolios: Avionics, Mission Sensors, Weapon Systems, Electrical Systems, Glass Cockpit, Automatic Flight Control System, Systems Integration Lab, Technology Group, Flight Test Centre.

In 2012, after more than two decades at Helicopter R&D Centre, when on promotion, she went to Aircraft R&D Centre (where she was to become the first Chief Designer of UAV later); she discovered with surprise that there were almost no women heading a design group at that time. That made her ponder about why this was the case. She realized what created the magic at Helicopter R&D Centre was that there was a role model in Madam KN Malathi, who had joined in 1973, almost a decade before the younger women engineers arrived. Many women Engineers had joined this division in the 1980s, which was a critical mass for a positive chain reaction to occur.

The Woman who deserved

Madam K.N. Malathi was the first woman design engineer at HAL to join the organization as a design trainee in 1973. She became the first woman Additional General Manager (AGM) at HAL. At one time, she handled three essential responsibilities. She deserved to be the first woman Chief Designer and GM of HAL. But the glass ceiling was hard to break at that time. After her retirement in 2010, the next decade saw half a dozen women rise to CD and GM positions. Nemichandra became the first lady Chief Designer and the second lady General Manager at HAL.

Recognition for Women in Aviation

She was thrilled to see the 'Aero India International Show 2019' celebrate **'Women in Aviation'**. They were hailed as 'Queens of the Sky,' and 14 of them from the Army, Air Force, Navy, Coast Guard, Civil Aviation, HAL, NAL, DRDO, and ISRO were felicitated including Nemichandra recognizing their contribution to the field of Aerospace.

She says, "We have come a long way from the 'it's Barbie dolls for girls and Airplanes for boys' era."

Policy Intervention Required

She says 'we see SSLC results yearly, and headlines scream, 'Girls on top yet again.' In school, girls are on top. But where do they vanish later? Why do we not see them flooding the corporate circles, Board Rooms, or Research Labs?'

When Nemichandra was nominated to be on the Board of BAe-HAL Software Limited in 2013, she did a small study to realize that women on boards in India are less than 5%, while at the same time, the boards in Scandinavian countries had more than 35% women. Global studies have shown that a company functions well when diversity is on board. Policy intervention did help.

The Company Act 2013 mandated that 'all listed companies are required to have at least one woman director on their boards from 1 April 2015'. The percentage of women on boards in India in 2016 was 13.7%.

However, women cannot suddenly be in senior positions or in the boardroom unless recruited at entry level and prepared for leadership positions. Policy intervention to ensure gender balance while recruiting for entry-level posts would help.

Individual's Responsibility

Today, working women have better support systems than in the past. However, she is concerned when many brilliant young women in engineering choose the soft option of 'working from home.' It is great for work-life balance and okay for shorter durations.

However, she is worried that the doors opened with enormous effort and sacrifice by women of previous generations should not close again. Gender bias is very much a reality even today.

Shared with the permission of Nemichandra

"Resilience at Every Turn: Journey to the CMD's Chair"
R. Vidyarthi (Name changed)

(Graduated in 1983 – Retired as Chairman & MD– currently a consultant)

"Resilience in adversity is the significance of perseverance and strength."

"Adaptability and continuous learning are key to success."

"Networking and mentorship are invaluable in advancing one's career."

"Believe in yourself, even in the absence of external affirmation."

"Maintaining a work-life balance is essential for long-term success."

Rising Through Resistance – A Journey of Perseverance and Leadership

Success is rarely a straight path—it is filled with obstacles, resistance, and moments of doubt. For Vidyarthi, the pursuit of leadership was shaped by these very challenges.

A Dream Begins: Entering the Steel Industry

Vidyarthi worked for 31.5 years at a steel plant, starting as a Management Trainee (Technical) and rising to the position of General Manager across various departments. Towards the end of his service, he moved on to become Chairman and Managing Director of a different public sector company.

After completing his Master's, he joined the steel industry as a Management Trainee (Technical). This was like a dream come true for him, as the organization had a big name in the metallurgical Industry, offering the scope to climb to the topmost position—Chairman cum Managing Director.

Gaining Expertise in Continuous Casting

Vidyarthi was fortunate to be posted to the Continuous Casting Department, the latest technology at the time in the country. As part of his job, he was sent to the erstwhile USSR for six months for specialized training in operating a continuous casting machine. After returning from training, he got involved in pre-commissioning activities. In 1991, commissioning activities began. It was a challenging job requiring 12-14 hours of hard work, but he thoroughly enjoyed it, as each day brought a new problem to resolve. His timely promotions and appreciation from superiors validated his dedication.

First Encounter with Discrimination

In 1992, Vidyarthi felt, for the first time, that he had lost a promotion due to discrimination. To his surprise, his promotion was denied, while a colleague—who had been suspended for 2-3 days on the pretext of negligence—received one. Distraught, he considered resigning and going abroad to look for a job. That year, widespread resentment among many aspirants led top management to study flaws in the promotion policy. Recognizing the errors, they revised the system and backdated promotions to ensure impacted employees retained their seniority.

Exposure to Leadership and Management Skills

In 1994, against his will, Vidyarthi was made Technical Assistant (TA) to the Head of the Department (HOD). Despite the demanding nature of the role and the poor work-life balance, he gained exposure to managerial skills, business strategies, and interactions with top management. However, his visibility led to jealousy and restlessness among colleagues and immediate seniors who feared missing their promotion.

Upon successfully completing the assignment, he was made head of a crucial unit in Continuous Casting. Though his performance was exceptional and he introduced improvements, past jealousy from seniors led to humiliation and insults. Still, his perseverance earned his next promotion, transferring him to a tougher and more challenging area within the department. He quickly adapted, applying his success strategies to the new role.

Facing Resistance and Overcoming Setbacks

Vidyarthi's innovative ideas started yielding results, yet they were met with resistance and non-cooperation from his seniors. Frustrated, he escalated the issue, only to face further humiliation.

Around this time, the Steel Plant was launching a new and innovative department—one perfectly suited to Vidyarthi's work ethic and aspirations. This new division aimed to drive organizational change by presenting cutting-edge ideas, new technologies, best HR practices, and marketing strategies directly to top management. There were no hierarchical delays—top executives would own and implement strategies.

A Major Turning Point: Entering a Strategic Role

Leveraging his familiarity with his previous HOD and the current Director, Vidyarthi requested a transfer to this new department. His reputation and demonstrated capabilities earned him the role.

This was a significant milestone in his career, bringing him close to renowned international organizations and senior officials from JSW, ESSAR Steel, Ispat Industries, TATA Steel, and SAIL. He had opportunities to visit their plants and learn about their work culture and technologies. He also became the coordinator for a board-level subcommittee, exposing him to the thinking and working styles of independent directors. Collaborating with top management to identify new technologies and automation systems, he felt at the peak of his professional growth.

A Sudden Fall: The Dismantling of His Department

Every growth story has setbacks, and Vidyarthi was no exception. When leadership changed at the top, the new brass dismantled the innovative department, dismissing its value simply because it was created by a previous regime.

Vidyarthi was transferred to an insignificant department with no challenging work, leading to frustration and sleepless nights. This difficult phase began to take a toll on his health.

Determined to Reach the Top

The humiliations, frustrations, and resistance from seniors while executing good work fueled Vidyarthi's determination to occupy the top positions in public sector organizations. Exposure to top management and independent directors gave him insight into how to apply for leadership roles and prepare for interviews. He resolved that one day he must either be a CMD or a Director of an organization to showcase his full potential.

Applying for Public Sector Leadership Roles

With encouragement from his close friend, Mr. Rao, Vidyarthi pursued leadership positions despite the systemic biases—regionalism, casteism, and other factors that influenced promotions. Mr. Rao continuously motivated him, urging him to apply for Director/MD positions.

After attending 5-6 interviews, in Vidyarthi's words, "securing these roles was not an easy task without either 'pull' or 'push.' My 6th interview with a big company was the final straw, and I decided to stop applying for public sector undertakings altogether."

An Unexpected Call: The Defining Moment

One evening, around 6 PM, as he was wrapping up his office work, Vidyarthi received an unexpected phone call from Delhi. The caller informed him that he had been shortlisted for the CMD position of a company in an Automobile Manufacturing Industry. She explained that since they had not received a sufficient number of applications, they were considering second-position candidates from previous interviews.

She persuaded him to attend the interview, assuring him that he could always skip it if he wished. After much deliberation, he attended—and to his surprise, he was selected as the CMD of a company in an Automobile Manufacturing Industry.

Shared with the permission of R. Vidyarthi

"Saving sight, shaping futures."
Dr. Subhadra Jalali

(MBBS – 1986; MS – 1989; currently Network Director at LVPEI)

"Women need to understand how men think and accept that we are different."

"Work with love, conviction, focus, and passion!"

"Life is precious and beautiful—enjoy it by making it full of joy for others around you."

"No shortcuts, no hanky-panky, pure spiritual worship to your work and womanhood."

"Balance is about prioritizing what truly matters."

Breaking Barriers, Transforming Lives – A Pioneer in Retinal Surgery and Newborn Eye Care

Medicine is not just about treating diseases—it is about innovation, persistence, and changing lives. Dr. Subhadra Jalali's journey reflects this philosophy.

A Journey of Excellence in Ophthalmology

Dr. Subhadra Jalali (Kaul) pursued her MBBS from Government Medical College, Jammu, in 1986, followed by an MS in Ophthalmology from PGI Chandigarh in 1989. She then completed a two-year fellowship at L V Prasad Eye Institute (LVPEI), Hyderabad, in 1993, further refining her expertise with short-term fellowships in the USA in 1995 and 1998. Her specialization in treating premature born babies with acquired retinal problems and those with genetic eye diseases set the foundation for a groundbreaking career. At a time when retinal surgery was an exclusively male domain, Dr. Jalali became one of the first women in India to enter this field in 1991. Possibly the second full-time trained female retinal surgeon in India, she defied societal expectations and carved a niche for herself.

A Global Leader in Newborn Eye Care

Since 1993 she has served as a Retina Consultant and is currently the Network Director overseeing 'Quality activities and accreditation' of more than 300 eye care centers of LVPEI network. In addition, as the Network Director. As the Network Director of Newborn Eye Health Alliance (NEHA), she has played a pivotal role in advancing neonatal eye care. Her contributions extend beyond surgery—she has delivered 1,100 scientific lectures in over 30 countries, authored 250+ peer-reviewed publications, and actively engages in public awareness through print, TV, radio, and social media.

Training the Next Generation of Retinal Specialists

Dr. Jalali's crowning achievement is the training of 350+ fellows in Retinopathy of Prematurity (ROP) and newborn eye diseases worldwide—the first such hands-on program globally. She also conducted the first-ever surgical workshop on infantile retinal diseases, pioneering advanced techniques in this niche field.

Her efforts have led to one lakh ROP babies receiving care across the LVPEI network, and she has established similar programs in multiple cities and countries.

Overcoming Bias and Breaking Stereotypes

When she applied for a two-year fellowship in retinal surgery, she faced skepticism and outright discouragement. She was told that women were not suited for retina surgery, that she would struggle with maternity leave, and that her long hair would be an obstacle.

Her response? A confident smile and the words: "Thanks for the welcome; I hope to make you change your mind about women."

Her mentor, Dr. Taraprasad Das, initially doubted her ability but later became her strongest supporter and lifelong guide. His mentorship helped her navigate challenges, secure international training, and establish herself as a leader in the field.

Navigating Leadership and Gender Perspectives

Dr. Jalali's career progression has been on par with her male colleagues, with no discrimination in medical and research opportunities. However, she observed that leadership dynamics often differ between men and women. While she did not perceive systemic bias at LVPEI, leadership remains male-dominated, influencing certain aspects of career growth. Over time, she adapted to these realities, choosing which aspects to align with and which to remain true to herself.

Redefining Work-Life Balance

Unlike conventional views on work-life balance, Dr. Jalali sees life as a seamless integration of work, family, and passion. Inspired by the women in her family, she embraced a holistic approach to managing responsibilities.

She implemented strategic parenting techniques, such as:

1. Living next to the school to minimize travel time.
2. Aligning her children's schedules with hers, ensuring quality time together.
3. Outsourcing routine tasks to focus on values, storytelling, and emotional security.
4. Maintaining strong relationships with family members for a supportive network.
5. Reading extensively on childcare and relationship management to refine her approach.

A Life of Passion, Energy, and Engagement

Dr. Jalali has never compromised on her passions, including dancing, travel, and social work. Her efficient time management and networking allowed her to integrate all aspects of life seamlessly.

She actively engages with all cadres of staff, whether sharing a meal with housekeeping staff or attending high-profile banquets. Her genuine love for people has made her a respected figure in both professional and social circles.

Lessons for Women in Leadership

She believes that women's leadership is often hindered by:

- Lack of organization and efficiency in managing life's responsibilities.
- Failure to build excellence in multiple skills through focus and hard work.
- Unclear vision for a meaningful life journey and self-empowerment.
- Misunderstanding how men think, leading to unnecessary comparisons instead of embracing unique strengths.

Despite societal limitations, she was fortunate to have **strong foundations in values, spirituality, courage, and education**.

Continuous Learning and Growth

Her only regret was not focusing earlier on emerging technologies, financial literacy, boardroom dynamics, and communication efficiency. However, she continues to learn and evolve, ensuring that future leaders—both men and women—are equipped with the skills to succeed.

Dr. Subhadra Jalali's journey is not just about medical achievements—it is about breaking barriers, inspiring change, and redefining leadership. Her contributions to newborn eye care, mentorship, and gender equality have left an indelible mark on the medical field, paving the way for future generations of women in ophthalmology.

Shared with the permission of Dr. Subhadra Jalali

"Balanced by Design: A steadfast Journey of Leadership and Life"

Meera K.S.

(Graduated in 1984.; Retired as VP of an IT company in 2021)

"As women, we have extra parameters to work with as society accepts/admires women working in our time."

"Balance is identifying which deserves the most attention and tilting to the side that deserves the most attention."

"Dream big and negotiate your way up. Don't give up on something you don't believe in."

"Happiness comes from the intersection of what you love, what you're good at, and what the world needs."

"Develop a great sense of humor. Have a hearty laugh at the end of the day."

"Nobody is a threat to me nor am I to anyone"

Navigating Dreams, Choices, and Change: A Journey of Growth and Balance

Meera's journey is one of resilience, adaptation, and unwavering determination. From her early aspirations in engineering to navigating the evolving landscape of India's IT sector, she continuously shaped her path while balancing societal expectations and personal ambitions.

Beginnings and Aspirations

Meera did her Electrical Engineering from UVCE, Bangalore. The course was five years long. When she did her engineering studies, the education system was different. They had very few engineering colleges. Our economic situation was in line with other countries, i.e., minimal options. She had dreamed of becoming a software engineer. She was intrigued by that field. There was social apprehension about women getting into Engineering and staying in a hostel away from home for safety.

The initial part of her life in engineering college was managing changes in life related to staying away from home, creating a safety net, and self-management. She made friends and was introduced to living with friends from various backgrounds. This was a phase of self-discovery. In her view, it is a MUST for all students to stay away from their parents to experience this.

Five years in Engineering taught her "how to be a fish in a pond." Hostel life honed different types of humor, which set the stage for what was to come.

Navigating Career Choices and Shifts

Initially, she resisted joining the public sector, feeling that it would be self-restricting as she aimed for product development. She worked for a software product development company and went through different ideation processes for starting her own company. But after working for those years, she realized that *"Kuch Paane ke liye bahut Kuch Khona Padtha hai."* (To gain some, we need to lose some). Starting a company requires a lot of money and success is uncertain. As a middle-class household, it is involved with risk. Hence, she decided to take up a job instead of starting a company.

India was warming up to the Services era when developed countries started recognizing its potential, offering work that involved cutting-edge breakthrough technologies. This economic shift led her to join HAL, a public sector company.

In the initial part of her career, she worked in the public sector as part of Computer Services (IT wing) for 10 years, focusing on automation aspects and the company's future needs. She did not experience any significant gender-based challenges; closed appraisals applied to everyone. But felt closed appraisals were suffocating and it was applied to everyone. In closed appraisals, employees do not get to see manager's comments post the appraisal.

Embracing the IT Sector

She joined an IT company in February 1997. For the last 23 years, this IT company has been her second home. She has been part of various departments, with opportunities in critical roles. She never felt left out.

At that time, working in IT meant adapting to a different pace of communication—there was no access to emails at home, so employees had to visit the office for international calls and email deliveries, waiting for customer acknowledgment. Calls had to be taken from the office. Technology was evolving at a much slower pace compared to today.

Remaining relevant became essential. *"One must also run oneself as a project at any time."* She focused on self-training, mentorship, and evolving alongside the ever-changing industry.

She managed many large accounts and travelled to different parts of the world to coordinate with customers. She grew from middle management to senior management level and became a member of senior management team.

She faced a number of challenges during her career, dealing with tough customers, toxic managers and complicated situations. She was the project manager for a Netherlands-based customer. Her team developed a series of products for the customer. He was very demanding and was always complaining. Finally, she agreed with him and told him, "I will give you fully tested products in the next two weeks. Please note that you must respond within one week if any changes are required. If you do not respond within a week, the project is deemed closed." Taking a stern stand and delivering a bug-free code, she successfully closed the project.

For another Australian-based customer project, there was a situation where the project was grossly under-estimated. It was initially quoted as a fixed cost project, but the scope kept changing with each delivery. She reasoned it out with the customer and made him agree to change it to time-based billing from a fixed price one. This change was a big victory, as she achieved 5 times the revenue of the original one for the company.

She had a perfect sense of humor and excellent conversational capabilities. She developed warm friendships with many customers. She used to negotiate well and get customers to agree to her terms in many cases.

She views challenges as necessary for personal completeness. Choices at each stage of life come with trade-offs, and one must embrace both merits and demerits of the selected path rather than dwelling on the benefits of roads not taken.

She often illustrates this perspective with a hospital analogy—some outpatient cases are treated like ICU patients, while some ICU cases are handled like routine OPD appointments. Hence, understanding priorities and addressing them accordingly is key.

She had a few rules to navigate opportunities and maintain balance:

(a) Not a superwoman
(b) Outsource as much as possible
(c) Restrict yourself to things that you alone must do
(d) Be judicious in time allocation
(e) Never compromise on family time
(f) Connect with fulfilled friends and groups
(g) Build bridges, not burn them

(h) Deal with things with an open mind and foster openness around you
(i) Use dignity, empathy, and grace in diverse situations
(j) Give back to others in all circumstances

Balancing Career and Family

The initial part of her career was low-keyed, keeping her daughter in view. She was not willing to travel and took up assignments without travel. It was a compromise, which she fondly remembers. She left that constraint after her daughter was old enough and started traveling.

In her view, "As women, we have extra parameters to work with as society accepts/admires women working in our time. But along with other house-related responsibilities, it was not either or but both. Families prepare their daughters to enter professions but often forget to prepare everyone in the household to redefine their roles in this new context. The responsibility of balancing work and home thus falls entirely on women, as questions like 'How do you manage both?' are rarely asked of working men."

Navigating Bias and Workplace Realities

At different stages of her career, she encountered biases—both self-imposed and external. She firmly believes that cultural and social biases should be addressed consistently rather than conforming to unnecessary expectations.

Women faced hurdles in networking, as professional men were unprepared for mentoring female leaders. Unlike their male counterparts, women were rarely included in informal guidance sessions and leadership conversations.

Embracing Growth and Self-Belief

Reflecting on her journey, she identifies key lessons she would have embraced earlier: (a) Fearlessness (b) Openly confronting challenges and closing issues decisively (c) Acknowledging success and strengthening self-belief.

She defines balance as focusing on what deserves the most attention while remaining egoless in situations where giving is required.

Final Reflections

She says, "None of us got stuck in the 1st Standard. Remain confident. Dream big and negotiate your way up. Don't give up on something you don't believe in. Become a 'bad loser.' Happiness comes from the intersection of what you love, what you're good at, and what the world needs. That's all balancing is all about. Operate like, " No body is threat to me nor I am threat to anyone". Finally, develop a great sense of humor. Have a hearty laugh at the end of the day. Because that takes you all the way happily."

American Philosopher Henry D. Thoreau said, "You cannot dream yourself into a character: you must hammer and forge yourself into one." [3]

Grasping Systemic Barriers

Nemi has worked hard persistently to remove gender biases in all spheres of her life.

Vidyarthi's case study gives a threadbare the kind of power-play that are experienced in big public sectors.

Meera, in her conversation with me, mentioned inner circle vs. outer circles in organizations, and despite the best results, some are relegated to the outer circle only. Nemi spoke about gender biases and how it impacts women.

Figuring Out Systemic Obstacles

Organizational culture, which comprises unsaid rules that tell people how to behave at work, is often the cause of systemic barriers. These rules can make places where certain people, ideas, or points of view are pushed to the edges. It's noticeable that the same point, when voiced by a female colleague, often receives a different response than when expressed by a male counterpart. Unfair practices like biased hiring and promotion processes, limited access to mentoring, and unequal leadership opportunities worsen these problems. Many of the successful women in the case studies were upset that they weren't considered for leadership positions even though they were qualified, which shows how common these problems are.

Systemic hurdles have a big effect on organizational effectiveness. Because of them, it can be hard for diverse employees to get promoted, and there aren't enough people of different backgrounds in top positions, because of which diverse inputs will not be there. This keeps gender discrimination going and makes it harder to come up with new ideas. Also, workers who feel left out or undervalued often have lower morale and less work gets done, which affects how well the team does as a whole. The first step in addressing these problems is to be able to sense them.

How to Handle Power-play at Work

Power-play at work has a bearing on how people's careers develop. Research shows that women are more likely than men to be sensitive to gender bias and how it affects them at work. One study by LeanIn.org and McKinsey & Company showed that women are more aware of biases and how they affect the workplace. Even though many women are aware of this, they feel less confident in handling office power-play well. Harvard Business Review wrote that women are less likely to promote themselves, which can make them less visible and less effective.

To deal with these situations, it's helpful to know how the organization's power works. Find the important people who make decisions, have an impact, and act as casual leaders in the workplace. Informal communication channels, commonly known as the "grapevine," can also give you helpful information about how a group works. Another good approach is to make friends across departments. Working with people who share your values and goals can help you build a network of support that can help you handle problems better. For instance, you could tell a coworker, "I like the way you're handling X." "Would you be willing to share tips on how to deal with problems in this area?" can help people connect meaningfully.

Getting Rid of Gender Bias

Biases based on gender, stereotypes, and social training often keep women in the background, which limits their chances to grow and lead. Women must actively work on giving themselves more power and fighting these biases. One way to do this is to keep track of what you've accomplished. Keeping track of your contributions, appreciations, and successes can help you show that you are competent when people are skeptical or biased. For example, when faced with preconceived notions, using facts and results to show competence can be powerful: "In my last job, I was in charge of the Y project, which led to Z outcome. I can get the same results here."

It's important to become highly trustworthy within the organization. Comparing yourself with coworkers and questioning based on that is not a good idea. Instead, think about your successes and abilities. Looking for a guide or a sponsor can also help with advice and support.

Getting rid of stuck ways of thinking

Personal biases and beliefs that limit viewpoints are often the cause of fixed ways of thinking. The first step toward having a more open mind is to be aware of these biases. Actively looking for and listening to different points of view can help you question what you believe and gain a better understanding. To make this process easier, teams should be encouraged to talk to each other freely. For instance, making forums where workers can talk about their problems and experiences can help people understand and care more about each other.

Another critical step is to encourage a growth attitude. Innovation can happen when people see problems as chances to grow and encourage others to leave their comfort zones. Supporting a culture of always learning, where trying new things is welcomed, and failure is seen as a way to improve, can help this thinking even more. For example, recognizing times when different points of view led to good results can help people see how important it is to be open to everyone.

Methods for Getting Past Systemic Obstacles: Actionable Tips

1. Advocacy and Awareness

Role of individual:

Create a Support Network: Develop informal network among peers. Participate in HRBP meetings, one-on-one's and skip level meetings – attend different forums that regularly meet to discuss achievements and challenges, amplifying each other's voices.

Document Success Stories: Collect success stories from these groups to highlight their contributions and bring them to management's attention.

Document Unsaid biases / hidden fears: Collect unwanted developments that may be happening at different parts of the organization and bring them to management's attention. Speaking out against unfair practices and backing projects encouraging 'diversity and inclusion' can help enhancing positive work culture.

Role of Management:

Role of senior leaders and policy makers: They need to be sensitive to the organizational culture and any systemic barriers that are getting cultivated. Encourage behaviours like: If you find any systemic barriers, you must raise them and advocate for the affected person. This will give you a lot of credibility and create a healthy work atmosphere.

2. Navigating Workplace Power-play

Role of individual:

- **Understanding Power Dynamics**: This needs the ability to sense the happenings around. First off all, all employees should know the Org chart, decision making process and decision makers in the organization. As an employee, one must learn this through training sessions or by going through the documents available for Org structure and processes. In addition, there will be informal leaders who influence the key decision makers. One should be cognizant of this and understand this also.

Role of Management:

Role of senior leaders: If they come across any informal leaders and manipulators in the system, they need to take stern action and discourage such behaviour.

3. Addressing Gender Bias

Role of individual:

Self-Advocacy: Women need to track their accomplishments and prepare to present them confidently during performance reviews.

Seek Mentorship: Seek mentorship programs where experienced professionals can guide those facing gender biases. Provide mentorship to juniors and others who are in need.

Role of Management:

Advocacy by senior management: Women leaders in senior management need to work towards sensitizing on systemic barriers for women. Need to support by making the management see their contributions. At the same time, sensitize women colleagues to be professional and equi-footed in their asks.

Policy changes: Identify the policy changes required to make the workplace Diversity and Inclusion compatible. Implement POSH and other similar forums to make the workplace safe for women.

4. Challenging Fixed Mindsets

Open Dialogue Forums: Establish regular forums where employees can share experiences and discuss biases openly, fostering a culture of understanding.

Growth Mindset Workshops: Implement workshops that encourage employees to view challenges as opportunities for growth, helping to shift fixed mindsets.

5. Implementing Change Initiatives

Conduct Surveys: Regularly survey employees to identify systemic barriers and areas for improvement, using the feedback to inform policy changes.

Set Diversity Goals: Establish clear, measurable diversity and inclusion goals within the organization, ensuring accountability at all levels.

Devise doable plans: Changing how company hires people, starting mentoring programs, giving diversity training, or setting up a 'grievance redressal forum'

Conclusion

It's important to break down systemic barriers and question fixed ways of thinking at all levels, to make the workplace more open and creative. Organizations can make real change by recognizing how these barriers affect them, encouraging a growth mindset, and implementing strategic projects. Accepting differences and promoting open communication make employees more engaged and help the company succeed. People and companies dedicated to removing these barriers make it possible for creativity, teamwork, and growth to happen at work. A proactive approach is needed to deal with office power-play and biases. By using these methods, we can make changes and set new policies where everyone has a chance to do well.

Exercises

1. Draw a map of how your workplace works – **workplace dynamics map.**

Step 1: Make a simple org chart of your workplace and list the people who make decisions, have a lot of power (formal/informal), and work with you.

Step 2: Write down any possible biases or political problems you've seen, like favoritism or a lack of diversity in leadership.

Step 3: Come up with a plan to get around these problems. For instance: Make friends with people who can speak up for you.

To fight bias, write down your accomplishments. Find teachers who have been through similar problems and come out on top.

As a bonus activity, work on your "strategic visibility" by joining high-impact projects or groups and showing off your skills to important people.

2. Next Exercise:

Add a "Support Network" layer to your org chart when you're mapping out how things work in the workplace. Find: People who can help you as **mentors**; **Sponsors** who can speak up for you in places where decisions are made; **Peers** who can help each other feel better and share their thoughts.

3. Bias Awareness Exercise:

Think of a time when you (or anyone else) felt ignored or treated poorly. Note down what took place. How did you feel about it?

What you could do better next time, like speaking up or writing down what you contributed. This makes you stronger and helps you find ways to fight bias.

4. Growth Mindset development:

A **growth mindset** is the belief that you can develop your abilities and intelligence through hard work, learning, and persistence. For example:

- **Fixed Mindset**: "I'm just not good at math."
- **Growth Mindset**: "I can improve my math skills with practice and effort."

Reader's Feedback

- Which story from the above stories is closer to your own situation?
- Do you have any additional ideas for overcoming systemic barriers?

CHAPTER 3

BUILDING A ROBUST NETWORK AND MENTORSHIP

Establishing a strong network and strategic relationships is crucial for career progress in today's times. This requires working on a personal brand, contributing to current trends, and actively connecting with superiors, peers, and subordinates.

All the leaders in this book expressed their networking abilities or lack of such abilities and consequences of it. A select few are presented in this section, where this aspect is demonstrated more dominantly than others.

"Empowering minds through creative design and critical thinking"

Dr. Gayathri Aaditya

(PG in 2006; PhD 2016; Currently Principal of Sir M V School of Architecture)

"Leadership is about making tough choices."

"Work smart, not just hard."

"Build strong networks and seek mentorship."

"Take bold leaps and stay curious."

"The glass ceiling may exist, but competence, vision, and fearless decision-making can shatter it."

Redefining Leadership—Architect, Educator, and Entrepreneur

True leadership is not confined to titles but is reflected in the ability to innovate, inspire, and adapt. Gayathri's journey exemplifies this mindset—spanning architecture, urban planning, academia, research and entrepreneurship. From pioneering sustainability in design to spearheading educational reforms, she has consistently challenged conventions and embraced growth. Her path is defined not by gender expectations but by resilience, strategic vision, and an unwavering commitment to excellence. Through mentorship, institutional leadership, and industry collaboration, she continues to shape the future of education and entrepreneurship, proving that success is built on competence, not convention.

Early Foundations in Design and Urban Planning

Gayathri's journey began in design, working with a firm immediately after earning her architecture degree from Andhra University (2004). Seeking broader horizons, she pursued graduate studies in Urban and Rural Planning at IIT Roorkee (2006), which set the foundation for her passion in sustainable development.

A pivotal moment came when she was accepted for doctoral studies at IISc, specializing in Sustainable Built Environments. This research-driven experience deepened her understanding of the intersection between planning, policy, and sustainability, culminating in her Ph.D. in 2016.

She then transitioned into academia, joining Nitte School of Architecture as an Associate Professor. Within a year, she spearheaded the launch of a Bachelor's in Planning degree, navigating the complexities of government approvals to make it a reality. Her research contributions were recognized when the Indian government awarded her the prestigious BHAVAN Fellowship, which took her to LBNL(Lawrence Berkeley National Laboratory), USA, for postdoctoral research (2018).

Returning to India, she focused on bridging the industry-academia gap through collaborative research, while shaping academic governance as a member of the Board of Studies and Examinations at Visvesvaraya Technological University. Her leadership extended beyond academics—she took on marketing and admissions responsibilities while heading the Planning department at Nitte. After serving as Dean of Research at Nitte, she transitioned to a new leadership role as Principal of Sir M V School of Architecture, continuing to drive innovation in education, research, and institutional strategy.

Entrepreneurship and CEO Leadership

Driven by an entrepreneurial spirit, she was selected into the first cohort of Entrepreneurs First, where she took a three-month sabbatical to refine her vision. This led to her venture into mindset training and learning assessments, integrating psychology and education to enhance metacognition.

As her startup's only female founding member, After years of navigating diverse roles in academia, research, and entrepreneurship, she realized that while technical expertise and policy frameworks are essential, true transformation begins with mindset. REAL Foundation was born out of this insight—a deep need to nurture Resilience, Empathy, Awareness, and Leadership in individuals and institutions.

Throughout her journey—from launching new academic programs to bridging the gap between academia and industry—she noticed that what often held people back wasn't a lack of talent, but a lack of clarity, confidence, and the courage to make bold decisions. REAL Foundation emerged as a platform to address these gaps—not just through training, but through deep, reflective processes that empower people to think critically, act mindfully, and lead with purpose. she was unanimously entrusted to lead as CEO—an affirmation that leadership is about vision, execution, and resilience, not gender.

In a world where the glass ceiling still exists for many, she has been privileged to operate in an environment that values competence over convention. She is committed to fostering similar opportunities for others.

Competence Over Convention—Navigating Leadership Without Gender Barriers

She has been fortunate not to have faced discrimination in her career due to her gender. Instead, she has been recognized for her ability to solve complex challenges, earning a reputation as a trusted troubleshooter.

Her leadership was valued not for her gender but for her ability to navigate uncertainty, strategize effectively, and drive results—making her a key figure in shaping institutional processes and mentoring future leaders.

Work-Life Balance—Efficiency and Structure

Work-life balance has never been about choosing one over the other but about optimizing both through efficiency and structure.

She prioritizes work efficiency and streamlined processes, ensuring that every task serves a purpose. Rather than spending long hours mindlessly, she focuses on high-impact work and avoids meetings without a defined agenda.

While work is significant, family is irreplaceable. She has always ensured that her loved ones remain a priority, even in difficult choices, such as her postdoctoral research at LBNL, USA, which required her to leave her two-year-old behind in India for a year—a decision made possible by the unwavering support of her family.

She delegates where necessary at home, ensuring that essential tasks are managed efficiently while personally taking charge of cooking to provide nutritious, wholesome meals for her family.

Networking and Learning from Senior Leaders

She deeply values networking with senior management as a catalyst for career growth and a vital learning opportunity. These interactions provide insight into strategic thinking, leadership, and long-term decision-making.

Beyond professional advancement, networking serves as a tool for resilience, allowing her to build meaningful relationships that provide guidance and critical feedback during adversity and high-stakes problem-solving.

Defining Leadership—Lessons for Aspiring Women Leaders

Success, for her, has never been about a single defining moment but about a **mindset** rooted in **resilience, strategic thinking, and the courage to take decisive action**.

Some of her key lessons for aspiring women leaders include:

- **Master the Art of Saying No** – Leadership is about making tough choices and avoiding distractions or unsustainable expectations.
- **Work Smart, Not Just Hard** – Prioritize meaningful work, set up structured processes, and hold yourself and others accountable.
- **Build Strong Networks & Seek Mentorship** – Professional relationships provide learning, resilience, and strategic insights during challenging times.
- **Embrace Leadership Beyond Titles** – Leadership is not just about positions—it's about creating impact, shaping institutions, and bridging industry-academia gaps.
- **Balance with Purpose, Not Guilt** – Prioritization and strong support systems make career and family coexist meaningfully.

- **Take Bold Leaps & Stay Curious** – Growth comes from stepping into uncertainty with confidence and conviction.

Shattering the Glass Ceiling with Competence and Vision

The glass ceiling may exist, but competence, vision, and fearless decision-making can shatter it. Leadership is not about fitting into a mold—it is about defining and confidently owning your path.

Shared with the permission of Dr. Gayathri Aaditya

"Law is her language, leadership her legacy."
Smita Priyadarshini

(Graduated LLB in 1999, currently Sr. Director at BCG)

"Do what you love doing and give nothing less than 200%."

"Women need to let go of the 'guilt complex' for not being around full-time for their children."

"The most important duty one owes is to oneself."

"Building a reputation for excellence, reliability, and a strong work ethic is crucial."

"Finding mentors and sponsors in a male-dominated industry is challenging but essential."

Breaking Barriers, Building Legacies – A Trailblazer in Law and Leadership

Success in the legal profession demands more than expertise—it requires resilience, adaptability, and a commitment to driving change. As a seasoned lawyer and leader, Smita has consistently defied expectations, challenged biases, and shaped the future of legal operations.

A Visionary Leader in Law and Business

Presently Senior Director and Executive Legal Counsel at Boston Consulting Group (BCG), she is an experienced lawyer and leader with extensive in-house and private practice experience. With a proven track record of advising senior executives, leading successful teams, and delivering service improvements and cost reductions, she has spent 25 years shaping the legal profession in the information technology and services industry.

In addition to a law degree, she holds an Executive MBA and a degree in education, uniquely positioning her to leverage technology to drive productivity gains in the legal profession. Her journey has been marked by strategic leadership, adaptability, and a commitment to excellence.

Previously associated with Dell for more than a decade, she supported several regional portfolios and managed a team of lawyers handling commercial transactions across the US, EMEA, and APJ regions. She played a key role in developing India as a cost-effective location for the legal function and successfully led the Contracts and Legal as a Shared Service (CLASS), which houses several lawyers based in Delhi and Bangalore providing support to various global regions.

Before Dell, she was associated with Perot Systems, where she headed the legal department of TSI (India) Private Limited and served as the lead counsel for the Asia-Pacific region. During her tenure, she was a Director on the Board of TSI India. She joined Dell as part of the Perot acquisition in 2009.

Prior to Perot Systems, she worked with Luthra & Luthra Law Offices, a premier law firm in India, where she led teams handling privatization, disinvestment, and the IT sector.

Championing Women's Rights and Workplace Equity

She has led several women and employee-related initiatives at her various organizations and has served as the Chairperson for the Sexual Harassment Redressal Committee. Passionate about women's issues, she has delivered lectures on various legal topics and was instrumental in establishing a foundation to serve underprivileged populations in India.

She has a valuable piece of advice to Women in Law on carving their Niche and owning their Value.

With only 15% of practicing lawyers in India being women, gender imbalance remains a significant challenge. Systemic barriers, cultural norms, and institutional biases have historically impeded women's progress in law. She believes gender diversity in the legal profession requires a multifaceted approach, including better mentorship for female lawyers, flexible working arrangements, and policies that actively promote inclusion. Encouragingly, law schools in India have seen a rise in female enrollment, and the appointment of women to high-ranking judicial positions signals a shift toward gender parity.

She believes the legal profession offers immense opportunities for women to shape careers, influence societal norms, and contribute to justice. Specializing in a legal niche can set women apart in a competitive field, and she has successfully carved out her own expertise. Capitalizing on opportunities in legal technology requires adaptability, continuous learning, and a strong professional network. Her advice: **Never underestimate your value, and don't let impostor syndrome hold you back.**

Balancing Career and Family – A Personal Perspective

Married to an IPS Officer and a mother of two daughters, she acknowledges the challenges of balancing a demanding career with family responsibilities. She believes that women must let go of the "guilt complex" of not being around full-time for their children, emphasizing that quality of time matters more than quantity.

The demanding nature of the legal profession makes work-life balance particularly challenging. She emphasizes setting clear boundaries, prioritizing tasks, saying no to non-aligned responsibilities, and learning to delegate effectively.

Further, she advocates for self-care, stating that while one owes a duty to others, the most important duty is to oneself. A fulfilled and contented individual can spread similar feelings of contentment. Her personal motto: "Do what you really love doing and give nothing but 200 percent."

Leadership Challenges

As a woman in a traditionally male-dominated industry, she has faced stereotypes questioning her competence and leadership ability. She overcame these biases by proving her capabilities through high-visibility projects and building a reputation for excellence.

She credits role models like Indira Jaising, a leading advocate for women's rights, and Aruna Roy, a champion for the right to information, as sources of inspiration. Beyond public figures, her career has been shaped by mentors within the legal profession and peers who have challenged, supported, and inspired her.

Finding mentors and sponsors in a male-dominated industry can be difficult, but she stresses the importance of seeking guidance and establishing a strong professional network.

A Legacy of Strength and Advocacy

Her journey is a testament to resilience, leadership, and the pursuit of excellence. By breaking barriers and building legacies, she has not only shaped her own career but also paved the way for future generations of women in law.

Shared with the permission of Lawyer Smita Priyadarshini

"A life in Science: Reflections and Lessons"

Dr. Ambuja Udas

(MSc 1976, PhD 1983)

"Women feel intimidated by male colleagues; self-doubt, systemic barriers, and biases."

A Life in Science: Reflections and Lessons

When asked to reflect on her life and career, Ambuja agreed, hoping that her story might offer guidance, reassurance, and perhaps even inspiration to young women navigating their own life journeys. What follows is a personal narrative of growth, discovery, and quiet perseverance—an account of how a young girl from Mumbai grew into a dedicated scientist and a thoughtful mentor

Early Years: An Unfolding Curiosity

Born as the first daughter to loving and supportive parents, Ambuja was raised in Mumbai, the dynamic commercial capital of Maharashtra. Her childhood was full of opportunity—good schools, access to arts and sports, and a nurturing home environment free from academic pressure. She recalls a happy, well-rounded upbringing where she was encouraged to explore her interests freely.

At one point, she was drawn to the culinary arts and seriously considered attending catering college. The idea of working in a kitchen fascinated her, and she had even procured the college prospectus. But the commute—12 kilometers with no direct bus—proved impractical. Instead, she enrolled in a science college nearby, a decision that would redirect the course of her life.

Unexpectedly, she found herself captivated by science. Subjects like physics and chemistry offered answers to everyday phenomena—why onions cause tears or how chocolate is tempered. That fascination with the how and why of things took root and never left.

The Making of a Scientist

Her growing interest led her to pursue a PhD under the guidance of an exceptional mentor—a scientist known not only for his academic prowess and up-to-date knowledge but also for his unwavering integrity. In his laboratory, she learned that research is rarely linear; it demands patience, persistence, and a deep work ethic. He fostered an environment where curiosity was encouraged and ethical conduct was non-negotiable. His mentorship had a lasting influence on her, so much so that in moments of difficulty, she often found herself asking, What would he do?

A Career in Public Science

In 1981, she joined a government research institution, where she worked until her retirement in 2014. Her career progression involved a mix of time-bound and interview-based evaluations. Some promotions arrived early, while others came on schedule, and a few arrived after delays. Regardless of the timeline, she viewed each stage as a chance to learn and evolve.

Her work was varied and deeply fulfilling. She supported departmental research initiatives, managed laboratories, collaborated with other scientists on interdisciplinary projects, and mentored younger scientists. She also attended national and international conferences, published papers, and regularly applied for grants to fund innovative research.

But she also recognized a disconnect between the scientific community and the general public, particularly among students. To bridge that gap, she organized science quizzes and elocution contests at colleges to demonstrate that science is not just relevant but thrilling. Her goal was simple: to motivate students to consider careers in science as vital to national progress.

Those 33 years, she often says, were among the most rewarding and meaningful of her life.

Lessons Along the Way

Over time, she encountered unique situations that offered life lessons—some surprising, others affirming. Here are a few she chooses to share:

1. Women Supporting Women

Contrary to the common stereotype that "women are women's worst enemies," her experience has been quite the opposite. She received tremendous support from women, both at work and in her social circles. She believes women often form strong, nurturing support systems and act as mentors for one another. In her view, it is maturity—not gender—that determines how people treat each other.

2. Let Your Work Speak

There were times when her scientific insights were questioned. Rather than taking offense, she responded with quiet determination, relying on consistent, quality work to speak for itself. Over time, this persistence won respect.

3. Striking a Balance

Balancing work and personal life was never easy. Her weekdays were long and intense, but she made a point of never missing family functions or important social events. This balance was made possible by a reliable support system at home and dependable colleagues in the lab.

4. Her Core Principles

Through the ups and downs, a few guiding principles emerged:

- Ask for help – Reach out to the right people and the scientific fraternity.
- Take responsibility – Growth often begins outside the comfort zone.
- Communicate clearly – Express intentions, expectations, and ideas with confidence.
- Build on a strong foundation – Integrity, skill, and depth matter most.
- Be realistic – Ambition should be tempered with perspective.
- Let go of the outcome – She doesn't believe that free will alone determines success. Her mantra became:

"Do your best and let go of the rest."

In Conclusion

Ambuja believes that meaningful growth—both personal and professional—stems from a willingness to step beyond one's comfort zone and to seek out purposeful collaboration. She views unfamiliar challenges not as obstacles, but as opportunities to learn, adapt, and evolve.

Her message to young women is this: Life doesn't always follow the path you plan—and that's often where its beauty lies. Stay curious. Be resilient. And trust that every detour and every challenge contributes to your unique and meaningful journey.

Shared with the permission of Dr. Ambuja Udas

"From Circuits to Solutions, a European Odyssey." Ravi C

(Graduated in 1987; Working overseas as a senior manager for a multinational company.)

"Success is not final, failure is not fatal: It is the courage to continue that counts."

"The only way to do great work is to love what you do."

"Family support is invaluable in achieving success."

"Cultural integration takes effort, but it is worth it."

"Resilience and adaptability are key to navigating challenges."

Resilience, Adaptability, and the Pursuit of Excellence – A Journey from Engineering to Leadership

Success is never a straight path; it is filled with challenges, sacrifices, and moments of self-doubt. Ravi's journey is a testament to the power of perseverance—an engineer who started in electrical systems and evolved into a senior leader in software and project management.

A Passion for Engineering Sparks a Lifelong Journey

Ravi's fascination with how things worked began in a small town nestled among rolling hills. His parents nurtured this curiosity, but it was his college Physics and Mathematics teachers who truly ignited his passion for Electrical Systems. This burning desire led him to pursue a degree in Electrical Engineering, setting the stage for an extraordinary journey.

His first job as an Electrical Engineer at I.T.W Signode, a Cold Rolling Steel Manufacturing Plant, felt like being thrown into the deep end. The plant was a maze of complex Electrical Drive Control Systems, presenting frequent technical challenges. The workdays were long, often stretching late into the night, leading to missed family dinners and bedtime stories read over the phone to his daughter.

His wife, however, was his rock. She understood his passion and shouldered a disproportionate share of family responsibilities, allowing him to focus on mastering the complexities of the plant. Winston Churchill's words resonated with him: *"Success is not final, failure is not fatal: It is the courage to continue that counts."*

Specializing in Electronics Engineering – A Balancing Act

After a few years, he decided to specialize in Electronics Engineering. Balancing work and part-time studies was tough, demanding careful time management. His daughter's innocent questions about his absence made these sacrifices even more challenging, but his wife's unwavering support kept him going.

His efforts paid off when he landed a job as Senior Maintenance Manager (Electrical & Electronics) at a leading Cold Rolling Steel Manufacturing Company. He lived by Steve Jobs' words: *"The only way to do great work is to love what you do."* But with greater responsibility came greater demands on his time, increasing pressure and stress.

His passion for Drive Control automation led him to explore PLC (Programmable Logic Controller) controls. He pursued additional courses and certifications, mastering the field. This opened doors to industry-wide recognition and sparked his interest in Software Programming.

Relocating to Germany – Professional Growth Meets Cultural Challenges

Transitioning to a Software Developer role in Germany was a turning point. While professionally rewarding, the move was challenging—adjusting to German work culture, climate, and language barriers added new complexities. His wife faced isolation, struggling to integrate into the local community, while their daughter adapted to a new international school.

Determined to overcome these obstacles, he enrolled in intensive German courses and encouraged his wife to join expat communities. Slowly, they found their footing.

His journey took an unexpected turn in Norway when he was offered a role as a Functional Consultant. With no prior experience, he embraced the challenge. The move was demanding, with further disruptions for his family. His ability to understand both technical and business aspects made him successful in this role, enhancing his career outlook. Having led SAP projects across continents as a Lead Functional Consultant, he aspired to become a Senior Software Solution Architect. His dedication paid off, earning him recognition as an expert in designing innovative solutions at Siemens.

Steve Jobs' words echoed his experience: *"The only way to do great work is to love what you do."* But this time, he added his own addendum: *"...and to have a family that loves and supports you through it all."*

Lessons from Mentors – Words That Shaped His Journey

Throughout his career, Ravi was fortunate to have mentors who shaped his perspective. One mentor, Mr. Paul N, advised: *"Never be afraid to fail. Each failure is a lesson that brings you closer to success."* Another, Mr. Thomas M, reminded him: *"Your ability to adapt and learn quickly is your greatest strength. Use it to your advantage."*

These lessons proved invaluable, helping him navigate the complexities of career transitions and family challenges.

A Legacy of Leadership and Lifelong Learning

His leadership abilities paved the way for his promotion to Senior Project Manager, overseeing mission-critical projects. His career trajectory—from Electrical Engineer to Senior Project Manager—exemplifies resilience, adaptability, and lifelong learning.

His name has become synonymous with industry excellence, and with over 25 years of experience, his journey offers invaluable insights for aspiring professionals.

Shared with the permission of Ravi Chakravadhanula

Building a Robust Network and Mentorship

Here are important factors to keep in mind when crafting your networking approach.

Personal Traits and Brand Development

Smita Priyadashini stresses the importance of seeking guidance and establishing a strong professional network.

Gayatri emphasizes the need for meaningful, deep connections rather than superficial ones.

Ambuja Udas received little support from her department, but with the help of her friends in other departments and her networking skills, she succeeded in her projects and funding initiatives.

Vidyarthi had a strong mentor who guided him through all critical situations.

In today's social media and the world of 'likes 👍', brand building is a vast subject. Everyone must have a social media presence, website, portfolio, etc. Here are some pointers on how to establish a personal brand.

Networking & Branding techniques

Building Your Personal Brand: A Comprehensive Guide

Being self-aware is the most essential part of personal branding. You can focus on doing what you do best if you know your skills, weaknesses, opportunities, and threats (SWOT). For instance, Sonali said, "By putting in place sustainability programs at Bry-Air, we cut the company's carbon footprint by 2." This shows what she's done and builds her reputation as an expert.

Setting SMART Goals

To effectively shape your personal brand, consider using the **SMART goals framework**. This approach helps you set clear objectives.

Action Steps:

- **Specific**: Define what you want to achieve. For example, "I want to increase my LinkedIn followers by 25%."
- **Measurable**: Determine how you will track progress. Use analytics tools to monitor follower growth.

- **Achievable**: Ensure your goal is realistic. A 25% increase should be based on your current growth rate.
- **Relevant**: Align your goals with your career objectives. For instance, "Increasing my online presence will help me connect with industry leaders."
- **Time-bound**: Set a deadline. "I will achieve this within the next three months."

By setting SMART goals, you can create a focused action plan that drives your personal branding efforts.

The 3 Hs: Hand, Head, and Heart Coordination

The coordination and alignment of Hand, Head, and Heart bring a lot of value to whatever you do, creating consistency in how you act, talk, and work. Over time, this builds trust and authenticity, making your brand easy to recognize and believe.

Setting Up Influence and Recognition

Building a name takes time and is based on doing a good job and being honest. You are being watched all around, which determines your character, so your work must match your values. To increase your impact, you need to earn respect, get more followers, and become better at convincing people. It's just as important to highlight accomplishments. I, for example, always took on complex tasks on my own, which showcased my skills and made me a trustworthy leader. Client feedback, manager appreciation, peer suggestions, or public sites like social media can all lead to recognition. All of these ways help raise your image and credibility.

Making Connections with a Goal

It's not enough to collect contacts; networking is about making genuine relationships. Jane showed this by setting up meetings with managers and coworkers independently, even though she sometimes got turned down. It's essential to get out of your comfort zone. For example, Meera started small by setting up casual coffee talks. Over time, she took two or three coworkers to lunch once a week to get to know them better. Setting limits is also very important. Saying, "I'll go to the team dinner, but I need to get ready for work tomorrow," shows that you can balance your job and personal life.

Building connections takes time and work. Saying things like, "I've always admired the way you lead," shows respect and asks for advice. "Could I get your help?" builds respect for each other. Making a collaboration map helps you find important people or groups to work with, leading to more productive partnerships. Strengthening relationships through casual get-togethers, like team birthday parties once a month, keeps the bond alive. You become a thought leader by sharing what you know, like when you give a talk called "Key learnings from my current project."

Finding Chances to Make Things Better

Leaders stand out because they are bold. You show initiative by finding the best way to handle challenging scenarios and suggesting solutions. Working together across departments and collaborating with different people without being asked to, shows you care about the company's success. Finding ways to improve yourself and working on it regularly is the only way to keep growing.

Keeping a Positive Attitude

As responsibilities increase, stress is bound to arise, but it's important to handle it and not let it overpower you. It's important to find what works for you, whether that's meditation, spending time with family, or other habits. Keeping calm and positive in tough situations not only boosts your mood but also motivates your team. Positivity in leadership can inspire others and build your image as a strong and reliable leader.

The Power of Being a Mentor

Find a guide. They can give you great advice. In case studies, many leaders missed this chance, but today's leaders are more proactive. A guide/mentor gives you advice from a neutral standpoint, someone who is not in your situation, which can help you deal with problems and make better choices. Over time, you will have people looking for your advice and seeking your suggestions. This helps in giving more fulfillment and satisfaction.

Making Use of Technology

In this modern world, it's important to network online. Professional networks can help you stay up to date with the latest developments. Joining forums connected to your industry can help you become known as an expert and connect you with other professionals who share your interests. Keeping these relationships alive by talking to each other often and responding quickly builds trust and makes working together easier.

Becoming a Member of Specialized Groups in Your Area

You can meet new people and stay current on the latest trends by joining specialized groups. Being active in these groups will help you learn new things and make new connections. You should always be focused on keeping your skills up-to-date, which keeps you ahead in your field.

In Conclusion

One must allocate time and effort to develop one's unique identity (brand) and network. You can get known and impact by focusing on self-awareness, consistent presentation, and strategic networking. Taking on challenges with optimism, looking for a mentor, and using technology can all help your career. Remember, building your brand is an ongoing process, not a one-time thing we do. You set yourself up for long-term success by constantly showing how valuable you are and taking care of your relationships.

Exercises

Exercise 1: Set SMART Goals for your personal branding

Exercise 2: Story bank and Own-pitch

Step 1: Create a Story bank with all your achievements and learnings. Include KPIs and make it quantitative so that it sounds authentic.

Step 2: Create a 30-second "elevator pitch" that highlights your significant achievements in a natural and authentic manner.

Step 3: Practice it by telling your close associates. Ask them if it sounds like boasting.

Additional Exercise: Fix lunch or dinner meetings with your close associates to exchange developments and ideas mutually.

Exercise 3: Create Collaboration Map

Step 1: Create a map of all key people with whom you need to collaborate for long term and short-term success.

Step 2: Schedule periodic meetings based on the periodicity required to maintain good relationship.

Step 3: Monitor the progress every quarter.

Exercise 4: Update your LinkedIn profile

Step 1: See your current LinkedIn profile, professional headline, elevator pitch. See if it is stating your personal brand correctly.

Step 2: Spend time to update your profile and to make headline more appealing.

Step 3: Share a post about your recent accomplishment to increase your visibility

Exercise 4: Create a social media posting calendar to achieve SMART goals

Step 1: Define the objective of social media postings. List down the subjects on which you want to post periodically.

Step 2: Create a calendar of when, which post, type of post, on which channel.

Step 3: Allocate some time of the day to work on the posts. Publish as per plan.

Reader's Feedback

- Which story from the above stories is closer to your own situation?
- Do you have any additional ideas for overcoming networking and mentoring?

CHAPTER 4

NEGOTIATION AND ASSERTIVENESS

In the workplace, negotiation and assertiveness are vital abilities that can greatly influence your career path. Mastering these skills enables you to effectively advocate for yourself, whether you are discussing salary increases, promotions, or overcoming obstacles. All the leaders in this book expressed their abilities in being assertive, negotiation – some dempnstrated and some haven't. A select few case studies are presented in this section, where this aspect is demonstrated more dominantly than others.

"Driving growth across borders with quiet force."
Nayeema Kouser

(ICWA in 2000 and IIMB in 2011; Currently Center Head at Sinch Cloud Communications)

"Hard work & persistence—there's no substitute."

"Success is about self-belief, not external validation."

"Take charge of your career—stop waiting for empowerment."

"Execution—great ideas mean nothing without action."

"You are only as good as you think you are. Own your journey, work relentlessly, and success will follow."

Owning the Journey: "She Didn't Wait—She Led"

When Nayeema Kouser walked into her first finance leadership meeting two decades ago, she wasn't just one of the youngest in the room—she was often the only woman. The air was thick with unspoken judgments, and every strategic suggestion she made was met with an extra measure of scrutiny. But Nayeema didn't flinch. She didn't wait to be empowered. She took charge.

"You are only as good as you think you are," she would later say. "Own your journey, work relentlessly, and success will follow."

Born with an innate drive to succeed, Nayeema's professional journey began with a deep focus on finance. She earned her Cost and Works Accountant (ICWA) certification in 2000 and went on to graduate from the Indian Institute of Management Bangalore in 2011—two powerful credentials that would help shape her unique blend of analytical rigor and strategic vision.

But her true education came through experience: two decades of navigating boardrooms, leading global teams, building capability centers from the ground up, and transforming complex financial operations across some of the world's most demanding organizations.

Today, as the Center Head at Sinch Cloud Communications, Nayeema is more than a finance leader. She is a transformation specialist, a talent architect, and a changemaker who has turned operational excellence into an art form. From finance and supply chain to data analytics, sales support, and procurement, she has built centers of excellence that drive tangible value for global enterprises.

But her path was never linear, nor was it smooth.

From Back Office to Strategic Leadership

Over the years, Nayeema played pivotal roles at global powerhouses like Kraft Heinz, AB InBev, State Street, Swiss Re, Juniper Networks, and Sun Microsystems. Each move wasn't just a step up the ladder—it was a leap across domains.

At Kraft Heinz, she was tasked with building and scaling a Global Capability Center (GCC) that would support functions from finance to logistics to data & analytics. It wasn't just about setting up operations—it was about reimagining them.

She drove cost transformation initiatives, implemented automation through AI and machine learning, and fostered a performance culture rooted in accountability. Her approach was always end-to-end: from P&L management to stakeholder engagement, from talent development to digital transformation.

Earlier, at AB InBev, she led Europe's finance and procurement operations. There, she spearheaded a 95% automation of account reconciliation, integrated Salesforce with SAP for seamless journal entries, and digitized vendor onboarding—achievements that delivered both financial and strategic returns.

At State Street, she managed global accounting and controllership functions across geographies like India, Poland, and China. And at Swiss Re, she served as a key partner in finance transformation, merging local expertise with global best practices to create sustainable impact.

But beneath the achievements was a deeper story—a story of pushing through walls few dared to name out loud.

Breaking Barriers, Boldly

Throughout her career, Nayeema encountered the quiet yet persistent obstacles that many women in leadership face: subtle biases, unequal pay, and the constant need to prove one's credibility in a male-dominated field.

"Early on, I realized that if I didn't raise my hand for high-visibility projects, no one was going to hand them to me," she reflects. "I had to step outside my job description to be seen as a leader."

There were meetings where her insights were only validated after being echoed by male peers. There were roles she was initially passed over for—simply because organizations assumed women wanted more flexibility and less responsibility. She negotiated for fair compensation when she discovered male counterparts earning more for similar roles.

But rather than let frustration take root, Nayeema turned it into fuel.

She built credibility through results. She silenced doubt with data. And slowly, the room stopped questioning why she was there—and began turning to her for the answers.

Integration, Not Balance

The myth of work-life balance never resonated with Nayeema. Instead, she embraced the concept of work-life integration, recognizing that leadership demands extraordinary commitment.

"I knew I couldn't do it all, but I could do what mattered—with intention."

That meant raising a self-sufficient son who today speaks proudly of her achievements. It meant having a partner who shared parenting responsibilities equally. And it meant carving out moments of deep, meaningful connection with her family—even when time was short.

She didn't strive for perfection. She strived for purpose.

The Power of Authentic Leadership

Nayeema is a leader who believes in **networking through impact**, not appearances. She doesn't believe in "playing power-play" or staying in anyone's good books for the sake of it.

Her leadership philosophy is simple yet powerful:

- Hard work and persistence—there's no substitute.
- Execution over ideas—because without action, vision is worthless.
- Self-motivation—because belief must start within.

She emphasizes storytelling—not just of one's achievements but of the value one creates. She teaches women to stop waiting for someone to hand them a platform. "Take charge of your career," she says. "Stop waiting for empowerment. Create your own momentum."

Perhaps her most controversial observation is that women don't always support each other enough. Too often, she says, women see each other as competition instead of collaborators. The result? Fewer women make it to the top, not for lack of talent, but for lack of solidarity.

"We don't need special forums. We need confidence—and we need to lift each other up."

Legacy in Motion

Nayeema's story is far from over. At Sinch, she is building the company's global strategy and shaping the GCC's identity not just as an operational hub, but as a business value creator. She's hiring people who are bold, who think big, and who want to build something lasting.

But beyond the titles and metrics, her legacy lies in the path she's cleared—for women, for global professionals, and for leaders who want to rise on their own terms.

"Success," she says, "isn't about validation. It's about believing you're enough—and doing the work to prove it to yourself."

In every challenge, Nayeema found an opportunity. In every bias, she discovered a deeper drive. And in every success, she made room for others to follow.

Her story is one of quiet power, relentless drive, and unwavering authenticity—a reminder that leadership is not given. It is claimed.

Shared with the permission of Nayeema Kuser

"Charting Her Own Flight: The Story of Grit, Grace, and Global Influence"

Padma C.

My story

(MTech in 1984; Currently serving as COO at Altumind)

"Never say no to any work that comes."

"Door openers could be small, but once it opens, grab the opportunity."

"Ultimate satisfaction in any work is only when end-users use it, and it stands the test of time."

"Women are not accepted as leaders because of the ingrained patriarchal thought process."

"I never wanted to compromise on career and related challenges."

Breaking Barriers, Building Legacies

In a time when opportunities for women were scarce, one girl defied the odds and changed the narrative forever. My journey wasn't just about career success—it was about breaking stereotypes, shaping industries, and proving that ambition knows no gender. From aeronautics to IT, from local projects to global leadership—this is the journey of a woman who never said no.

Born in the 60s, I was very brilliant as a student. When I cleared the Engineering entrance with a double-digit rank, which was not achieved by anyone in that town and by any known person, my parents decided to admit me into engineering. They had to face many questions on taking such a bold step with a girl child, but still, they went ahead. I went on to do B. Tech from NIT, Warangal and then MTech from IIT, Kharagpur.

Aviation Dreams and Early Career

My first nine years of work were at a public sector company (HAL) in the aeronautics industry. I joined there as a Senior Engineer. I was in the project that was to develop the latest technology helicopter indigenously. I had a great influence from my first manager, Malathi KN, a woman who was fiercely independent and versatile. Fortunately, I had the opportunity to fly in helicopters for avionics testing. I did very interesting work there. Presented a paper on "The Future of Helicopters" and won first prize for that. I grew up to the Manager level with regular promotions.

A Leap into Computers: Passion Meets Opportunity

Because of my interest and passion for computers, I requested for internal transfer and moved to the computer division at the earliest opportunity. The transition from aeronautics to IT was driven by my fascination for computer science, sparked by my exposure to technology in aerospace engineering.

One day, there was a bandh in the city. I was seven months pregnant, and that day I also ran to catch the office bus in the early morning. Then people in the bus stopped me from getting into the bus, saying that we do not know how the situation will turn out, you first go back to home. That was the level of commitment I exhibited throughout my career.

Balancing Career and Family: A Test of Endurance

Once I joined the computer division, I was made part of a customer project in an outstation. The entire team was new and not experienced in doing projects for external customers; every project used to be in RED, a very demanding customer, and unending working hours and days. My son was less than two years old. I used to carry him to outstation duties and leave him in my aunt's place. I used to get stuck in office with 'bugs', go-live, etc. This little kid used to wait for me on the balcony only, without eating food. My husband used to take care of the daughter at home.

Balancing motherhood and critical responsibilities and high-pressure situations on work front, I stood resiliently with the determination to never let personal challenges come in the way of my professional excellence. I developed a strong risk-proof support system to navigate challenges at home. At times, I had to part with my son from the fifth month to the tenth month, visiting him every weekend. Even though I developed a support system wherever I traveled, it remained tough, with the toddler waiting for me in unknown places.

Though there were questions in my mind on whether what I was doing was right, it never crippled me. I strongly believed that it was for my children's betterment—for them to have a good education and a bright future.

Another instance to demonstrate that I prioritized conflicts as appropriate to situations. Once I was in London, working towards winning a deal. Then a phone call comes saying that my Father-In-Law has passed away. The meetings were in a crucial stage and my absence would impact the order. Hence, I decided to prioritize office work over a personal emergency, continued my mission, and came back after a week with the order in hand.

Establishing myself in IT: Challenges and Triumphs

From HAL, I moved on to an IT company (Sonata Software) as a Project Manager. It was not easy to establish myself. At the junior and peers' level, proving myself as a software person was straightforward through handling show-stopper situations in complex technical areas. At the management level, my hard-working nature and result-oriented approach helped me establish myself as a software project manager.

A Defining Moment: The First International Breakthrough

My first project as a project manager was for a big international brand. To start with, it started as a small project for their India branch. It was done in 2-3 weeks using an upcoming code generator tool in those days. The following events were astounding. This small piece of software had attracted the attention of big bosses in the headquarters, in Europe. There came an invitation to present the application and the technical design there.

The defining moment is when my manager asked me, "Who can be a better person than you to go and do this job?" That was shocking to me as I had never travelled abroad, never presented in any big forums, and that was my first project as a PM. But I decided to plunge into action.

This bold step required deep preparation – understanding the international audience, detailed technical explanations that resonate with their expectations and ensuring an appealing presentation. On seeing my presentation and the application, they decided to roll it out across all countries. From a small project, it became a mammoth project with a multi-year maintenance contract.

Lessons from Growing Career

Here are a few takeaways from this experience:

- Never say no to any work that comes. If it is a business-critical application, in all probability, it will grow big.
- Door openers could be small, but once it opens, grab the opportunity.

- Make sure that whatever you deliver gets used. Ultimate satisfaction in any work is only when end-users use it, and it stands the test of time. End-users should fully own it and use it.

I gained many professional and personal skills like handling global customers and delivering applications end-to-end; Excellent experience in Project and program management; contracts and agreements; delivering quality code, and project cost management.

Expanding Horizons: Managing Global Programs

Due to the success of the project, my confidence grew multifold. The ability to travel, communicate, and influence people in other countries was quite challenging, yet satisfying. This has opened up bigger opportunities to lead large programs. Top management's confidence and trust in my abilities have increased, and it has opened floodgates into my career progression.

With this success, I got promoted as Program Manager for another big project, which involved managing teams from Europe, India, and the US. It involved extensive travel to different European countries. This enriched my knowledge and experience in dealing with complicated situations. Post that, as Delivery Director, I handled a few more similar large accounts in different geographies like Europe, the Middle East in addition to the USA. All these involved extensive travels to different parts of the world.

I grew to be a member of the key decision-making committee of the company, participated in the company's vision and strategy meetings, and is instrumental in the company's growth path. I was the only woman in that committee for many years. As the company has picked up on the growth path, lot of focus was required for taking care of internal systems and processes. I headed internal operations, achieved many statutory certifications for the company and implemented company-wide systems and processes.

Diversification and Lifelong Learning

I identified the need for an MBA qualification and pursued it despite my hectic career. I was also sponsored for training at IIMA and ISB to develop management skills. I diversified my expertise into organizational processes, Quality management & certifications, HR, recruitment, and other internal-facing management domains.

Navigating Leadership Challenges and Gender Bias

Managing multiple customers and team members, I faced many challenging situations. In some cases, there were genuine project delays or quality issues. I would travel to meet the customers in person and work out solutions. It could be a process issue, a technology issue, or just communication gaps. I was able to resolve many situations amicably by approaching the challenges with reason and logic and by being the leader on the ground.

Predominantly, up to senior manager level, execution abilities take precedence, recognition & promotions are directly proportional to one's contribution. Above that level, a glass ceiling exists for all, irrespective of gender, as the numbers are lower up the ladder.

But women have some additional setbacks: They are not accepted as leaders because of the ingrained patriarchal biases across all stakeholders: The board, managers, peers, subordinates, and customers.

At times, my assertiveness used to be quoted as aggression and argumentativeness. With that, I struggled with impostor syndrome, questioning my original confidence.

But I navigated through all these situations with grit and merit. Metrics and quantitative demonstration of results are the main principles that worked for my, along with being part of key and visible projects of the organization. I had many firsts in that organization, first woman to be promoted to senior manager level, one of the first few women to become VP. Many women in the organization often expressed that I was their role model.

Be+ - The Power of Positivity

I had a very smooth working relationship with the majority of female and male counterparts from the customer side. Due to all the ups and downs in different accounts and projects, I gained visibility in management. I was instrumental in winning many big deals for the company. I had immense patience and used to motivate the team not to be restless about results. "Be positive (Be+)" was my motto, and I influenced everyone around me on these lines.

Building a Personal Brand

I had not explicitly worked on personal branding, yet my presence and resilience established my reputation. Annual get-togethers in the company were memorable, bringing together employees and their families. On one such occasion, despite being injured with a broken leg, I attended the event with my family. My teenage daughter observed how people gravitated towards me and admired my strength, reinforcing the impact I had on others.

A Legacy of Strength and Vision

My silver jubilee function was celebrated with a big fanfare in a prestigious hotel, where I was acknowledged for all my contributions by the top management and all my peers. On my retirement day, most of my peers and managers, whom I mentored, spoke laudatory words about my 'never say die' spirit and accepting any job with open arms.

I realized that what remained with me was the success of the organization during my tenure and the moments of triumph at key milestones. Having spent nearly seventy percent of my active life with that organization, I cherish every moment that I spent with them.

"Refining Her Legacy: Breaking One Barrier at a Time"

Jane (Name changed)

(Graduated in 1983 – Retired in Senior Management cadre in Steel industry)

"If a woman talks loudly, she's branded as 'Aggressive.'"

"Work, family, and life are equally important. Because sometimes, you need to pause so you can truly move forward."

"Thriving women's mindset is to aim high and work relentlessly to reach their aspirations."

"Whatever you do—give it 100%."

"Step out of your comfort zone, get to know new individuals, find a mentor, and do what they're doing."

Jane's Journey in the Oil Industry: Breaking Barriers and Embracing Challenges

Early Career Beginnings

Jane joined as an Officer Trainee in an oil refinery and, after a year, was promoted to Technical Engineer. She quickly realized that very little of what she had learned in engineering college was applicable to refinery engineering. Her daily tasks involved monitoring process units and troubleshooting technical issues using computer simulations. Fresh graduates were trained to follow safety practices rigorously, and the facilities were awe-inspiring. Most workers were friendly and helpful, but Jane learned that in a factory environment, no one spoon-feeds your technical knowledge; individuals must work hard to acquire it.

As a woman engineer, Jane was part of a minority; in her B.Tech batch, there were only 7 women out of 265 students, and in the refining division, women comprised just 1% of the total engineering staff.

Career Progression and Challenges

Jane dedicated 27 years to the technical services of the refining division and spent an additional 10 years in Corporate Department. Her responsibilities included conducting audits in refineries, terminals, depots, LPG plants, and cross-country pumping stations, as well as developing training modules and best practices. She retired in a senior management cadre after 37.8 years of service, leaving behind a clean service record.

Throughout her career, Jane faced discrimination as a woman, often being overlooked for promotions in favor of less qualified male colleagues. Despite demonstrating strong performance and exceeding expectations, her commitment was frequently questioned due to assumptions about her potential family responsibilities. Instances of bias included being assigned administrative tasks not typically given to male colleagues, having her ideas dismissed as "too emotional," and receiving lower performance ratings compared to male counterparts for similar work. After taking maternity leave, she faced skepticism about her commitment to her job, which limited her advancement opportunities. Additionally, being a woman from a minority ethnic community further hindered her access to training opportunities offered to her colleagues.

Confronting Gender Bias

Jane encountered numerous instances of gender bias. When she requested a raise, she was told that she didn't need a good performance rating because "her husband makes good money" as part of a "double income couple." A male colleague once dismissed her solution to a problem as incorrect, attributing it to "female intuition." Later, he found the same solution, labeling it as "male rationality." Jane remarked, "If a woman talks loudly, she's branded as 'aggressive.'"

When a junior colleague became her reporting manager, he audaciously made vulgar comments about her to other junior colleagues while maintaining a facade of professionalism in front of her. Jane complained to PoSH committee and made sure that appropriate action is taken on the person.

Posh: The Sexual Harassment of Women at Workplace (Prevention, Prohibition, Redressal) Act, 2013 by Indian Government is commonly known as the PoSH Act 2013.

Work-Life Balance Philosophy

In the refinery environment, the culture often emphasizes relentless work, with colleagues prioritizing job performance over work-life balance. Most employees dedicated long hours to impress their superiors and secure promotions. Jane, however, prioritized hard work and sincere performance over the pursuit of promotions. She believed that work, family, and life are equally important and learned to balance all three. In her words, "Sometimes, you need to pause so you can truly move forward."

Once her workday was complete, she devoted time to her family, enjoyed walks, prayed, cooked, and managed household responsibilities, all of which contributed to her relaxation and happiness. Jane traveled occasionally, relishing these trips while keeping work thoughts at bay, returning motivated and energized.

Mastering Networking

She is systematic about networking with senior and junior management people. She used to manage the fine art of networking at both senior and junior levels by fixing their calendars ahead of time! She used to arrange a formal one-to-one meeting, and if they declined, change to the next available slot. She won't be put off if they don't attend. She had to hear "no" more than she would have liked to, but she took these setbacks gracefully. She was tenacious and had thick-skin attitude, which helped her come back stronger and more prepared next time.

On the flip side, where get-togethers were organized with an informal touch and a lighter note, she was cautious enough to be present yet chose to leave early before such occasions got hyperactive. In network meetings at the organizational level where majority are men, predators cannot go unnoticed or underestimated, and hence she learnt to be careful.

Advocating for Change

Jane believes that addressing gender bias requires implementing inclusive hiring practices, developing leadership programs tailored to women, and promoting flexibility in working hours and locations to create a more women-friendly workplace.

The "secret" of her career success has been hard work, self-belief, relentless pursuit of knowledge, networking, knowing her boundaries, sticking to her values, and a willingness to take calculated risks.

Jane's advice to aspiring women includes:

- Embrace your unique strengths.
- Actively seek mentorship and advocate for yourself.
- Be innovative and never shy away from challenging opportunities.
- Give 100% to whatever you do.
- Step out of your comfort zone and connect with new individuals.
- Find a mentor and learn from their experiences.
- Show up early
- commit to lifelong learning.
- Regularly review your career path and introspect on feedback.
- Practice tenacity and
- keep your promises.

"Thriving women's mindset is to aim high and work relentlessly to reach their aspirations."

Shared with the permission of Jane

"Engineering nourishment, leading with purpose."
Srinivasa Prasad

(Graduated in 1985 -VP/Technical Director)

"Knowledge is power."

"Soft attitude and situational leadership are key to success."

"Deep cooperation with all people is essential."

"Learning new things and sharing knowledge with others is crucial."

"Creating opportunities as required and making soft/hard decisions based on the situation."

From Challenges to Triumphs: A Journey of Resilience, Leadership, and Lifelong Learning in the Edible Oil Industry

Srnivasa Prasad's career is a testament to perseverance, adaptability, and strategic leadership. From his early days to leading large-scale plant operations, his journey reflects dedication and continuous learning. Over the years, he has faced industry challenges, corporate transitions, and workplace power-play, yet remained steadfast in his commitment to efficiency and ethical leadership.

Early Career Beginnings (1987)

Srinivasa Prasad started his journey in 1987 after completing his B.Tech in Oil Technology. His first challenge came at a Vanaspati and Solvent Extraction company, where he faced a competitive environment with 18 other candidates, young and experienced. As a fresh graduate who did not know Hindi, he felt at a disadvantage. The interview process began at 9:30 AM with a five-member panel, including a Government Officer. Srinivasa Prasad was the 12th candidate and endured a grueling 55-minute interview. Despite relying heavily on bookish knowledge, he successfully advanced to the second round, where nine candidates were selected. The second round was particularly tough, and he feared he would not advance, but to his surprise, his name appeared on the list of five selected candidates. The third interview concluded late at night, around 10:30 PM. Ultimately, he was one of two candidates selected for the position of Junior Shift Officer, serving in shift timings for three years

(1986-1989). During this tenure, he received two additional job offers but chose not to pursue them.

Significant Project Contributions

From 1990 to 1992, Srinivasa Prasad was selected for a position with the Maharashtra State government through the National Dairy Development Board (NDDB). He was one of the 14 core team members who got selected in Maharashtra government(MAHAFED), after 4 rounds of interview, it is a very prestigious position. Got this offer after working for 3 years in private organization in M.P. He was tasked with starting a project that involved the installation of a 1000 TPD edible oil Complex. Remarkably, they completed the project within nine months and successfully commissioned it before Srinivasa Prasad left in 1992. During this journey, he completed the DBM (evening college) from Pune University.

Following this achievement, Srinivasa Prasad secured a better opportunity as a Works Manager in another solvent extraction company in March 1992. His responsibilities included installation, commissioning, and his hard work did not go unnoticed. In 1993, he was promoted to Factory Manager, a position he held until March 1995.

In April 1995, Mr. Prakash Parakh, the honorable Managing Director of Parakh Foods and Oils Limited, invited Srinivasa Prasad for an interview based on the positive feedback he received about his work. He was appointed as the General Manager of plant operations, and during his ten-year tenure (1995-2005), the entire team developed a national brand "Gemini" and "Samrat", he oversaw a significant increase in plant capacity from 1200 MT to 3500 TPD across two states. Notably, he facilitated the first joint venture in an edible oil plant between his company and a US multinational giant, Cargill.

In 2005, he transitioned to the role of Plant Superintendent, managing operations in Orissa and Maharashtra (Parakh Foods). By 2007, he was promoted to Director of the combined entity, a position he held until 2014.

New Opportunities and Challenges (2014-2017)

As higher positions became saturated within the company, Srinivasa Prasad received an offer to join a larger plant as Vice President of plant operations. The Managing Director personally reached out to him to oversee four plants in India, where he worked from 2014 until March 2017.

In April 2017, he was called back by the Parakh group to serve as Technical Director of plant operations for three plants, a role he continues to hold today.

Navigating Power-play and Work-Life Balance

Throughout his career, Srinivasa Prasad encountered local political challenges, particularly with local MLAs who prioritized their associates for significant roles, often disregarding qualifications and efficiency. Whenever faced with such hurdles, situational leadership in unethical behavior and took a stand to confront it by going through the proper channels.

At various stages of his career, he had to compromise on family time to focus on work, although his family always supported him. From the year 2000 onwards, he achieved a better work-life balance and witnessed significant growth in his family life.

Insights on Networking and Mentoring

Srinivasa Prasad shares valuable suggestions for effective networking and mentoring:

Build Strong Bridges: Establish a strong connection between top management and staff through regular get-togethers and family functions.

Transparency and Communication: Hold daily meetings with Heads of Departments (HOD) and other staff to foster transparency.

Job Safety Awareness: Ensure all workers are aware of job safety protocols.

Positive Work Culture: Promote good planning, friendliness, and appreciation for quality work to enhance positive behavior among employees.

Collaborative Nature: Foster a cooperative and collaborative environment to motivate team members to build a comfortable working with a broad range of people.

Personal Philosophy

Srinivasa Prasad believes in the mantra, "Knowledge is power." His approach to leadership includes:

Soft Attitude and Situational Leadership: Adapting his leadership style based on the situation.

Deep Cooperation: Collaborating closely with all team members.

Continuous Learning: Emphasizing the importance of learning new things and sharing knowledge.

Acknowledgment and Appreciation: Recognizing and appreciating good work, fostering a culture of collective achievement.

Creating Opportunities: Developing win-win situations and opportunities as needed.

Effective Decision-Making: Making soft or hard decisions based on the situation and listening attentively to others.

Shared with the permission of Srinivasa Prasad

Negotiation and Assertiveness

Nayeema mentioned that she had negotiated and fought for fair pay without disparity between men and women.

Nemi's story shows the way she negotiated uncompromisingly in different aspects of women getting a fair share in different spheres of life.

Vidyarthi's case reflects that he was promptly following up and negotiating for his career growth. He gave an option before quitting, and then only quit.

Gayatri is very good at negotiation, and when things did not work out, she chose to switch the organizations.

Negotiating Salary Increases and Promotions

Planning is Very Important

Before starting any discussion, doing a lot of research is essential. First, look into the norms in your field to get an idea of the salary range for your job and the amount of experience. This information gives you a good base for your conversations. Knowing your worth is just as important. Make a list of your KRAs and value quantitatively delivered to the company. It should reflect your value to the company in business aspects as well as soft aspects.

When and how to act

Do not take this up when your chips are down or the company is not doing well. Take it up when you have achieved something significant or there is some big positive news around. Use precise, confident wording to make your case professionally. Keep a good mood and stress the importance of a win-win situation, pointing out how your growth helps you and the company.

Confrontational-ness without being pushy

Being assertive means making your wants known clearly and confidently without being mean. Find your key asks and give them to them honestly, focused on what you've done well instead of what others have done wrong. Listening actively is just as important, paying attention to what they say and answering carefully. Use "I" words to show that you own what you've done. Avoid saying "we" or "team"; you could specifically discuss your contributions. Being calm and composed, even when there is opposition, shows confidence, and the chances of arguments are lower.

How to Handle Setbacks with Grace

Sometimes, talks don't go as planned, and that's fine. Take comments seriously, whether it's good or bad, and use them as a chance to improve. Keep a way to keep track of your work so you can see where you need to make changes. Take losses professionally and dignifiedly, and don't point fingers or get into arguments. Recognize the feedback that helps you improve. Suppose it doesn't, remember that you can always choose another choice. Take some time to think about what went wrong and change how you negotiate in the future. This thought helps you understand things better and prepares you for the next steps.

Are you an essential part of the team?

How crucial is your role to the company? Is it a critical role in project completion? Is the customer trusting you well? Does it need the honesty and sincerity that others cannot meet with easily? Think about how much impact you have. Are your efforts necessary for important projects or initiatives to succeed? People whose skills and ideas greatly affect results are often mission-critical. Keep your knowledge up to date by learning new things and keeping up with changes in your field. This focused attention on where you are and how critical your role is for the organization and its growth has an impact on your growth path.

Ideal negotiation framework for Salary & Promotion

Interest Based Relational Approach is an ideal framework for salary and promotions. 1. Preparation, 2. Interests identification: Here along with your interests for hike/promotion you need show understanding about organization's interest and your value contribution for the growth. 3. Build Relationships: In addiiton to your contribution, talk about your manager's support and team's contribution; 4. Explore options: Ask questions, "If it is not possible to give immediately, can we come up with a plan for the same?" It could be time bound or achievement based, try to arrive at a plan.

In conclusion

Negotiation and assertiveness are difficult jobs but one must practice and develop these. You can become an important and valuable group member by doing your research, speaking confidently, and dealing with setbacks with grace. Building your brand as an expert in area of your expertise can help you get new jobs and have more impact. Use these skills in your job, and you'll see your work grow.

Actionable Tips

Write down your accomplishments: Write down what you've done and what you've accomplished. This is proof that you should be able to speak up for yourself. Use the "I-We-It" framework: Present your efforts in a way that makes them stand out. As an example:

I: "I was in charge of the group that came up with a new way to analyze trace elements."

We: "We cut the time it took to do the study by 30%."

It: "This fits our goal of making environmental analysis more efficient."

Get Ready for Pushback: Expect objections and prepare evidence-based answers to stay calm and professional during discussions.

Learn how to be assertive: If you are being mistreated or with bias, gently state your case. For example: "I understand your worries, but I think I'm a good fit for this job based on my history with my previous project."

Data can help you make your case: Show proof of what you've done to help with the talks. For instance: "Over the past year, I've been in charge of ABC projects that led to 30% reduction in cost." "I think I deserve promotion because of this."

Look for Win-Win Solutions: Try to achieve results that benefit everyone. For instance, "This strategy will help both the team and the organization if we implement it."

Find Allies: Look for top leaders or mentors who respect your work and can advocate for you. For instance, "I've been having trouble with this aspect. Could I get your help with how to handle this?"

Ask for Feedback: Asking for feedback from peers and managers will help you find ways to improve and show that you are committed to growth. When you use these strategies in your professional life, you can negotiate well, build a good name, and confidently move up in your job.

Exercise

Playing a negotiation scenario through a role-playing game

Step 1: Think of a time when you need to speak up for yourself, like when you want a raise, when you want to pitch a new idea, or when you need more resources.

Step 2: Write down your main points, focusing on the value you bring (for example, "I've consistently surpassed my goals, and I think this contribution warrants a salary adjustment").

Step 3: Act out the talk with a friend or teacher. Even if the other person pushes back, practice keeping calm, sure of yourself, and polite.

4. Think about what you did in the role play. What did well? What could you do better?

As an extra challenge, use the "I-We-It" framework to help you make your case. In a nutshell, make it give and take. Mutually beneficial proposals click well in negotiations.

Self-Advocacy and Goal Setting:

1. Make your manager understand your career goals
   In your next one-on-one meetings with your manager, share a goal you're working toward and ask for their advice on how to achieve it.
2. Advocate for Yourself Without Apology
   Practice framing your accomplishments naturally.
3. Set Realistic Goals and Celebrate Progress
   Break big challenges into smaller, manageable steps and celebrate each small wins.

Reader's Feedback

- Which story from the above stories is closer to your own situation?
- Do you have any additional ideas for demonstrating Negotiation and Assertiveness?

CHAPTER 5

WORK LIFE BALANCE

Managing work-life balance and setting priorities

All leaders in the different case studies dealt with in some detail on this subject. Ambuja Udas had a good support system. Abha had to struggle as a single mother. Jane explained how she allocates time for breaks. Vidyarthi's story brings out the need for taking breaks and relaxing, to avoid stress impacting one's health. Srinivasa Prasad explained the difficulties he had due to factories remote locations. Sonali explained the struggles as a single woman in completing household chores. Sunil and Ravi explained that the role of a spouse is to support their accomplishments. For Nemi a family function or even her book release was not a priority when it came to meeting her organizational demands. Meera said that she prioritized her daughter over work when the daughter was young, and she has no regrets for the same. Smita, Gayatri, and Nayeema proudly state how they balance their work and life. Very interesting advice from Dr. Subhadra in this area. She also gave a TED talk on this subject.

Finding Balance Between Personal Life and Career Goals

It is hard to find the right balance between personal life and work goals, especially in middle-aged brackets, as there will be hectic pressure from both the family and work sides. Here are some pointers about how to find a balance in this tricky situation.

Figure out your priorities.

Finding a good work-life mix starts with being clear on what's important. Setting clear goals for your personal and professional life can help you decide how to spend your time and energy. The **Eisenhower Matrix**[4] is a useful tool for this because it sorts jobs into groups based on how important and how quickly they need to be done. This method helps you figure out what needs your instant attention and what can wait or be given to someone else. For example, you might need to focus on a high-priority work job today, while planning a family trip can wait until the weekend.

Eat the ugliest frog first is one rule which helps in reducing procrastination. Ugliest frog represents the daunting, unpleasant or daunting task, which one is likely to procrastinate. This method says that you should prioritize it first and get it done when you have full energy. For eg., a very important client presentation is coming up. Ugly frog because of the anxiety associated and preparation required and presenting in front of every one. Schedule it as the first thing in the morning for preparing, practicing and being ready for the meeting.

The **"Top 3" rule** is another good way to think about things. Aim to finish the three most important things daily, whether personal or work-related. Making sure your to-do list is short and specific will help you feel less overwhelmed and make real progress in both parts of your life. For example, Ambuja Udas makes sure she leaves the office at 6 PM to catch the office bus, but she also lets people know she plans to finish chores early. She is clarifying that she is making time to complete pending work.

Setting aside time and making plans

Time blocking is a powerful way to keep things in balance. Setting aside specific times each day for work and meetings, family, personal activities, and self-care like exercise, walking, etc., helps you build a planned routine that keeps you on track and away from distractions. Like, you could set aside 9 AM to 12 PM for serious work tasks and 6 PM to 8 PM for family time. This method not only makes you more productive, but it also makes sure that you take care of your personal aspects.

It's essential to set time limits for each task. Have an estimate of how much time each task takes and try to complete it with minimal variation. The method, which calls for 55 minutes of focused work and then a 5-minute break, can help you stay on track and keep your energy up all day. For example, giving yourself time to relax from 7 to 7:30 PM before doing housework can help you feel refreshed and ready to take on the evening with more energy.

Learn how to decline well.

To keep things in balance, you need to learn how to say a firm "no." When your calendar schedule is full, turning down extra work or social requests is okay. In the same way, politely declining a social event that clashes with much-needed alone time can help you recharge.

When it makes sense, delegate.

Delegation is a key part of managing your time well. In Eisenhower framework, some of "Not important, Not Urgent" tasks can be delegated to others. Look for chances to share duties at work. Some jobs can be given to trusted coworkers, so you can focus on more important projects. You could ask a friend, "Could you take care of X task while I work on Y task? I'd really appreciate the help." When you're at home, splitting up chores with family or roommates keeps you from having to do everything yourself. If everyone is made to participate as per their strengths, equally, it works out very well.

Set up networks of support

For balance, it's important to build a strong network of support. Professionally, surround yourself with coworkers or mentors who can help and advise you. One example is that asking a guide for help when things get tough at work can help you handle the stress better. At home, do things like cooking, cleaning, and taking care of kids with the help of your partner, friends, or paid help. You won't have to do everything yourself if you ask for help when needed.

Put self-care first.

Taking care of your health (physical & mental) is important for a healthy life. It's important to include self-care in your daily life. Whether you work out, do sports, or just take some time to relax, these things will give you more energy and make you feel better overall. Setting clear limits between work and personal time is just as important. For example, turning off your work emails after 7 PM lets you do things with your family or yourself without interruption.

Be open to change.

Life is unpredictable, and strict plans can sometimes make things more stressful than they need to be. When you embrace flexibility, you can change when new needs come up. If work needs more time one week, you should change your tasks to fit, and the same goes for the other way around. Being able to change with time takes the pressure off and helps you keep your balance.

Develop a positive and strong attitude, quick wit

You can balance work and home life by having a positive attitude and looking at things in a lighter manner. Gaining a sense of humor and the ability to laugh even when things are tough can help you feel less stressed and have a better view of life. For example, narrating something comical in the middle of a tough work schedule with your coworkers can help ease the stress and make the workplace a better place to be. In the same way, being able to laugh off small mistakes at home, like a dinner that's burned or a drink that gets all over the place, can turn moments of anger into times of connection and joy. Having a quick wit not only helps you but also makes the people around you feel better, which makes the workplace and home more pleasant and peaceful.

Review and make changes often.

It's important to look at your work-life balance on a regular basis. Are you thinking about work too much? Is your personal life not getting enough attention? By checking in with yourself on a regular basis, you can find flaws and fix them. If work consistently interferes with family time, you must find ways to reduce the work pressure.

Smart use of technology

Technology can be both good and bad for work-life balance in this modern age. Use productivity apps and tools to get things done faster and better control your time. One example of project management software is that it can help you remember due dates and work well with others. But remember that technology can make distinguishing between work and personal life hard. To avoid being on call all the time, set times to check your emails and texts.

Have a growth mindset.

Developing a growth mindset can help you deal with the problems when you try to balance work and home life. Instead of seeing losses as failures, look at them as chances to learn and develop. For example, in a stressful situation like something has gone wrong in a project, consider what you can learn and how to do better next time. This resilience and flexibility are essential for staying balanced in a changing world.

In conclusion

Drawing a balance between your work goals and your personal life is an ongoing process that mandates one to be on top of things, continuously planning and changing the plans on the fly. You can live a full and balanced life with a dependable support system. One can never achieve a perfect balance; it's about making choices that align with your goals and ideals. You can handle the pressures of work and personal life with ease and confidence. Building a positive and strong mood will help you do well, and you'll be sure to find balance and enjoy the journey along the way. Smart use of technology and encouraging a growth attitude are two more things that can help you keep this balance in a world that is always changing.

Exercises

Exercise 1: Create Eisenhower matrix and list tasks in four quadrants.

Eisenhower Matrix (Urgent-Important Matrix) [4]

Overview:

The Eisenhower Matrix helps you categorize tasks based on their urgency and importance, allowing you to prioritize effectively.

Quadrants:

1. **Urgent and Important**: Do these tasks immediately.
2. **Important but Not Urgent**: Schedule these tasks for later.
3. **Urgent but Not Important**: Delegate these tasks if possible.
4. **Not Urgent and Not Important**: Eliminate or minimize these tasks.

Example:

- **Urgent and Important**: Project deadline due tomorrow.
- **Important but Not Urgent**: Long-term strategic planning.
- **Urgent but Not Important**: Interruptions like emails or calls.
- **Not Urgent and Not Important**: Social media browsing.

Workout: The Plan for the "**Ideal Week**"

Step 1: Write down top priority items for the week. For example, "Spend quality time with family," "Complete a major project," and "Exercise three times a week" are all things that should be at the top of your list for both work and personal life.

Step 2: Write down these goals on a weekly schedule. Schedule time to do things for work, fun, and rest.

Step 3: Here are a few rules to protect your time: don't check email after 7 PM, and take a complete lunch break. In Work from home situations, strict log in time, lunch break time and log out time for work.

Step 4: Try your plan for a week and think about what went well and what didn't. Change as needed.

As a bonus, work on saying "No" politely. Write down a polite but firm way to say no to extra jobs that don't fit your current schedule. For instance: "I'd love to help, but I'm busy with X right now." Let's talk about this again next quarter."

Refinement: When you make your "Ideal Week" plan, make sure to include *buffer time** between jobs in case of delays or changes you didn't expect. It makes you feel better and helps you stay on track.

One more idea to attempt: **The "Energy Audit":** Keep track of how much energy you have during the day for a week. Note: -When you're in the mood to work; and -When you're worn out.

Use this information to plan to do essential tasks when you have the most energy and easy tasks, like answering emails, when you don't have as much.

Exercise 2: Maintain a Sense of Purpose

Connect your work to a larger purpose to stay motivated.

Example: "I work hard to provide for my family and create a better future for them."

Exercise 3: Include fun and quick wit

Incorporate fun and lighter moments in daily routine. Try to have a cheer leader in the team, who will keep the atmosphere lighter.

Exercise 4: Seek Professional Support When Needed

Don't hesitate to ask for help from professionals.

Suggestion: Consider reaching out to a therapist, coach, or counselor if feeling overwhelmed.

Exercise 5: Take Care of Your Physical Health

Have a set routine to maintain phusical well being.

Exercise 6 : Practice Mindfulness and Stress Management

Do daily journaling

Do meditation

Reader's Feedback

- Do you have any additional ideas for achieving Work-Life Balance?

CHAPTER 6

SELF ACTUALIZATION & SELF EMPOWERMENT

"From Frontline Warrior to Boardroom Strategist"

Sunil Khurana

(Graduated in 1983 –Currently serving as Executive Chairman)

"Honesty and hard work were the key pillars that helped build confidence, credibility, and trust."

"Shortcuts never lead to lasting success."

"Enjoy what you do—without that, the journey towards success becomes unrealistic."

"Never let the fire or hunger within you die."

"Building domain expertise is fundamental to a strong career foundation."

A Journey of Growth, Leadership, and Resilience

Sunil's journey is a testament to perseverance, adaptability, and strategic leadership. From his early days in medical device manufacturing to leading multinational corporations and eventually building a homegrown company, his career reflects the power of embracing challenges and leveraging experiences.

Early Career and Transition into Corporate Leadership

Sunil began his career after completing his engineering in 1983, starting in a medical device manufacturing company. However, he soon transitioned to IGE (India) Ltd., the marketing arm of General Electric (GE), where he focused on sales and marketing.

In 1990, when the joint venture between GE and Wipro Ltd. formed Wipro GE, he became part of its growth, contributing to its success until 2012, when he left after holding a senior position.

Embracing New Challenges and Entrepreneurship

He then joined Bharti Infratel, a cellular tower company, as Chief Operating Officer. However, when Goldman Sachs presented an exciting opportunity to build a medical device manufacturing company from the ground up, he saw it as the perfect moment to leverage his nearly three decades of experience.

Seizing the opportunity, he applied his extensive industry knowledge to establish a homegrown business. Sunil served in the role of CEO & MD of BPL Medical Technologies for nearly 12 years. Today, he is delighted with the results—his company has grown to employ 900 people, with two large factories, and has the potential to become the country's largest indigenous medical devices company.

In April 2025, he stepped into the role of Executive Chairman of the company to focus on guiding the strategic direction, overseeing key decisions at the board level, and mentoring and hand-holding senior leadership to ensure alignment with our core values and long-term vision.

Navigating Workplace Dynamics and Career Growth

Sunil considers himself fortunate regarding discrimination; he didn't face any significant barriers. However, there were times when individuals with less experience or caliber were promoted ahead of him. Fortunately, this was only a temporary situation, and over time, he was able to succeed and advance in his career.

Balancing Work and Personal Life

Maintaining a work-life balance was quite challenging during the initial 10-12 years of his career. In the early years, it felt like the survival of a fetus, with very few opportunities available.

He recalls, "Naturally, compromises had to be made on the home front, but I was fortunate that my wife managed everything exceptionally well." She took full responsibility for their sons' education, ensuring their studies were well cared for. Thanks to her unwavering support, he could focus on his career freely.

To put things in perspective, when he started his career in the early 1980s, India's economy was vastly different. Something as simple as getting a landline installed took nearly three years—unimaginable in today's world.

He is deeply grateful to his wife for managing their home resiliently and adopting an austere lifestyle when needed. "Her support made all the difference," he said.

The Role of Personality in his Success

His career can be divided into two distinct phases. The first was as a frontline warrior—undoubtedly the most demanding period, navigating challenges at the very foundation of the corporate hierarchy.

For him, honesty and hard work were the key pillars that helped build confidence, credibility, and trust within and outside the organization. He firmly believes that shortcuts never lead to lasting success. At this stage, pushing beyond limits was like investing in the future—laying a strong foundation was essential.

Sunil has always embraced a simple, open, and noncontroversial approach. Earning genuine trust at every level has been invaluable. He truly enjoyed this journey and believes that one's personality should remain consistent, ensuring that everyone perceives them in the same way. Staying away from controversy has also been a great asset in maintaining stability and focus.

As he worked at a branch location in the initial stages of his career, meetings with senior management were rare, typically happening just once a year! Hence, networking opportunities were non-existent.

His approach focused on building strong bonds with his team, often at get-togethers to foster camaraderie. Taking on challenging roles and embracing risks proved invaluable for his growth. Successfully handling unprecedented tasks with passion and determination strengthened his capabilities and laid the foundation for his career progression.

The Influence of GE and His Leadership Philosophy

He was fortunate to spend nearly three decades with one of America's best organizations, GE. Unlike the common perception about many companies, he never witnessed a capable individual being denied what they truly deserved.

He carried this philosophy into his current organization, striving to create an equally meritocratic environment.

Diversity and Inclusion in Corporate Spaces

One challenge, however, is that many multinational corporations (MNCs) tend to prioritize hiring high-potential diverse candidates under the pretext of promoting diversity, often providing them with better opportunities and flexibility under global norms.

That said, in his organization, he ensures that every capable individual is given equal—if not better—opportunities, especially for female candidates.

Respect for Women in the Workplace

In his experience, women exhibit exceptional sincerity and output, often demonstrating greater focus on work without unnecessary distractions. Moreover, he greatly respects how they balance professional and personal responsibilities, contributing not just at work but also managing their home, family, and children. Yet, when it comes to making sacrifices for the family, women often step back to allow their partners to pursue their careers. As a result, only a tiny percentage of women ultimately reach top leadership positions.

Keys to Success and Professional Growth

Sunil shares his secret of success as follows: (a) The most critical factor in achieving excellence is enjoying what you do—without that, the journey towards success becomes unrealistic. Therefore, always choose a job profile that genuinely excites and interests you. (b) Never let the fire or hunger within you die. Your drive and passion propel you to the next level. (c) Equally crucial is your work ethic—it ultimately makes all the difference. Even when no one is watching, your self-discipline and integrity shape your success. (d) Building domain expertise is fundamental to a strong career foundation. (e) Additionally, maintaining the correct behavior, practicing humility, and fostering an open and motivating work culture have been key traits that have helped him grow both professionally and personally.

Shared with the permission of Sunil Khurana

"Against the Odds: Turning Challenges into Triumphs"
Abha Saxena

(Began her career in mid 30s; currently Founder & CEO)

"Work-life balance was an alien concept to me throughout my career."

"I truly loved my work and found deep joy in nurturing and caring for my children."

"Confidence is a great asset to succeed in life. Keep learning continuously with each opportunity."

"Age is no bar; I started late and yet succeeded."

"Identify your passion and build yourself in that area."

Embracing Challenges: Abha's Inspiring Journey in IT and CSR

"Believe in yourself and all that you are. Know that there is something inside you that is greater than any obstacle." — Christian D. Larson

Abha embarked on her career journey relatively late, after spending nearly a decade in Germany, in her mid thirties. Upon her return, she found that the Indian job market had evolved significantly, with the IT industry booming and ample opportunities available. Lacking the necessary qualifications, she first equipped herself with the required skills and took on the role of Centre Manager at a private computer training academy. Recognizing the market potential of multimedia training, she was instrumental in establishing her organization as the first franchise centre of a Arena Multimedia (a well know software training brand Aptech Limited) in South India.

Her transition into software services marketing began when she joined a mid-sized IT company (Sonata Software), where she steadily progressed and was eventually entrusted with managing the company's German office and its largest onsite client. After several years in the IT industry, she ventured into marketing consulting, focusing on startup organizations.

A Passion for CSR

Driven by a long-standing interest in CSR, she began offering advisory services to corporations and NGOs. As she became more immersed in the social sector, she found it far more fulfilling and shifted her focus entirely to CSR consulting and NGO advisory services. This passion led her to join a well known Foundation (NASSCOM) as Vice President – Programs. While overseeing CSR initiatives and disability inclusion programs, she identified a crucial gap that underlies the reason, why people with disabilities were overlooked in corporate hiring. Although companies were keen to hire people with disabilities, they lacked the necessary know how support, and structured guidance to make it happen successfully.

Founding Social Equity Advisory Services

After two enriching years at that prestigious Foundation, she returned to consulting with a renewed focus on CSR and disability inclusion, founding Social Equity Advisory Services. Over time, she specialized in accessibility and disability inclusion services for corporations. Over the past decade, she has supported several large and mid-sized organizations in their journey toward disability inclusion. This period has been both profoundly fulfilling and personally transformative for her.

Navigating Gender Discrimination

Abha experienced bias in the workplace due to both her gender and her age, as she was older than many of her colleagues. There was a hesitation to entrust her with challenging roles, and she had to advocate for herself to secure them consistently. That said, one cannot overlook the fact that the role in a European country was offered solely based on her competence, which was a reassuring experience for her. Abha explains, "However, I encountered a paradox: I experienced a noticeable lack of guidance and support;

despite my skills, commitment, and hard work, this made it challenging for me to advance. This ultimately led me to leave the organization, searching for a better opportunity, only to find that similar challenges persisted everywhere." She states, "It is deeply disheartening that women continue to be viewed through the lens of preconceived notions and biases."

Carrying the dual burden of agesim and gender bias had been a daunting challenge throughout her career. Even during job searches, she was explicitly told that she was too old for specific roles despite her proven track record, relevant experience, and unwavering enthusiasm.

She remarks, "Work-life balance was an alien concept to me throughout my career." As a single mother raising two growing children, she shouldered the full weight of family responsibilities while navigating the demanding work environment of IT companies. Striving not to compromise on her professional or familial duties, she often found that the only thing she could sacrifice was her comfort and personal time.

Abha explains, "Managing the home front was challenging. Although I had part-time help and my children pitched in occasionally, the primary responsibility rested on my shoulders. There were days when the first time I honestly sat down was after returning home and settling into my armchair. Yet, I have no regrets. I loved my work and found joy in caring for my children. I always believed that cooking and tending to their everyday needs was the least I could do for them, especially as they grew independent and self-reliant."

However, she missed taking vacations with her children or carving out leisure time for herself. In the end, the fulfillment she found in both work and motherhood made the journey worthwhile.

The Importance of Networking

Abha rarely networked with senior managers or attend company gatherings, believing that hard work and the quality of work alone would be enough to advance her career. However, she often observed colleagues who were more socially active and maintained visibility with senior leadership often advanced faster, sometimes ahead of their turn. In hindsight, she expressed that she should have made more effort to engage socially with her managers and colleagues, but she never felt natural or comfortable.

She reflects on a mistake she now recognizes: whenever she faced discrimination or adverse reactions from others, her instinct was to walk away. Looking back, she feels she should have stood her ground, reasoned with others, and sought guidance from senior leaders who valued her work.

Lessons Learned

In her view, this is a common mistake many women make: "We often choose not to raise our voices against discrimination, instead opting to step away quietly. Somehow, we tend to lose confidence in our strengths—a mistake we shouldn't make."

Despite numerous challenges, her success was anchored in one unwavering force - her belief in herself. When she entered the IT industry, she had neither formal qualification nor prior corporate experience. What she did have was a deep confidence in her ability to learn fast, adapt quickly, and rise to the occasion — and that made all the difference.

She welcomed every new opportunity open arms, trusting her ability to make it work. Her approach has always been bold and fearless dive into the deep end and figure out how to swim, trusting her ability to take on whatever came her way, with the quiet confidence that she would not only succeed, but thrive.

This mindset has shaped her journey—taking bold leaps, learning along the way, and celebrating every victory with the firm belief that "I can do it, I will do it well, and I will win!"

Abha genuinely believes in the wisdom of the quote: "Believe in yourself and all that you are. Know that there is something inside you that is greater than any obstacle."

Her story conveys these lessons loud and clear:

- Confidence is a great asset to succeed in life.
- Age is no barrier; she started her professional journey late and yet succeeded. Yet her accomplishments stand as proof that age is no barrier to success.
- Say Yes to opportunities embrace them even though they are outside your comfort zone.
- Don't stay silent in the face of adversity; stay your ground; confront challenges head-on.
- Follow your passion - Discover what drives you and build yourself around it.

Abha's journey is a testament to resilience, adaptability, and the power of self-belief, especially women — to embrace their paths fully, to rise above limitations, and to believe that it's never too late to chase what matters.

Shared with the permission of Abha Saxena

"Rooted in sustainability, thriving in leadership."
Sonali Dutta

(PG completed in 1984– Retired as VP Corp. Affairs & HR)

"Adapting quickly and turning challenges into opportunities is key."

"Being respectful and polite often opened more doors than being aggressive."

"Hard work pays, and it did."

"Step out of your comfort zone. Good communication, knowledge, empathy, and continuous learning are helpful."

"Today, women have so many opportunities. Embrace them."

Sonali Dutta: Uncharted Paths, Adapting to Succeed

Sonali's journey has been exciting and continues to be so, with its share of uncharted paths and adapting to succeed. It is a tapestry of reinvention, resilience, and transitions. After retiring as a senior corporate executive, Sonali promptly turned to organic farming, using permaculture principles to operate her small farm in Sawantwadi, Maharashtra. Her connections to the corporate world remain strong—she is an advisor to several corporates, a mentor to many young professionals, and an Independent Director on the board of a company.

She is also a passionate sustainability advocate, serving as the National President of the Corporate Sustainability Council, WICCI, and a member of the National Advisory, G100 - Diversity, Equity, and Representation. After almost forty years of corporate life, of which over 33 years were with Bry-Air and the Pahwa Group (where she retired as Vice President of Corporate Affairs & HR), Sonali chose to step away from the security of her management position and the comforts of city life in Gurgaon. She semi-relocated to Goa near the agricultural land she acquired about a decade ago, wanting to grow it as a natural organic farm and offer a getaway to authors, birdwatchers, and others seeking a break from hectic city life. Her farm maintains its natural biodiversity and serves as an example of carbon farming through bamboo plantations. This decision was driven by a desire to lead a more sustainable life and leave a better planet for future generations.

A New Chapter: From Executive to Farmer

When she reached 60, the age at which many people retire, Sonali had the option to continue as an advisor in the corporate world but wanted a change. She relocated to Goa to be closer to her agricultural land in Sangeli, Sawantwadi. Leaving behind the comforts of Gurgaon, she sought a new venture that would test her physical and mental endurance.

For someone who had always lived and worked in urban areas, this decision required a lot of soul searching. Farming is not easy, but it can be fun with the right mindset to tackle unusual challenges. Fortunately, she had the moral support of her brother and on-ground support from a friend who owned and operated an adjoining farm. It took several years, but today her farm is truly sustainable, powered by solar panels and utilizing water from a well she had dug on the farm premises, allowing her to grow a mini-forest.

The terrain was unfamiliar, and village life came with a learning curve. For a person used to 24/7 power and backup in Gurgaon, the farm with no power connection, mobile signals, and running water required a significant mind shift and many adjustments. Gaining acceptability was another challenge; in her corporate life, respect came from capability and position, but here she was a stranger to the land, language, and village. Surprisingly, she gained acceptance when she started staying alone at the farm for weeks without rushing back to Goa for material comforts.

Sonali has now built her own cottage on her farm and is in the process of furnishing it. She gained the respect of the locals when they realized that she was always up for challenges and adventure—having driven her own car from Gurgaon to Goa and Sangeli. Now, she is well accepted and respected because, as her contractor constructing her cottage noted, she didn't talk down and always tried to learn from everyone. The challenges made her stick around, and she has started selling naturally grown organic produce in small quantities. While her main reason for shifting to Goa was to make the farm financially sustainable and lead a relaxed life, she has gotten involved in many other projects, each bringing the excitement of building something from scratch.

At 60+, Sonali rewrote the script of her life. She began learning pottery, embraced new business ideas, and found energy in building ventures from scratch. Reinvention became not just a response to life's changes but a deliberate way of life. What was meant to be a quiet retirement became another launchpad for a new way of life.

Early Choices and an Unconventional Start

After completing her post-graduation in Economics in 1984 from Chandigarh, she tried preparing for the UPSC and other exams, but her heart was not in a stable bureaucratic job. Determined to take up a job in the private sector—encouraged by her supportive parents—she joined the workforce at the right time. In the mid-80s, India was embracing new technologies, from high-end telecom switches to personal computers.

Sonali's professional journey began in 1985 with a detour. Her first job was with a market research firm, where she worked as a field executive, collecting survey data from various socioeconomic groups. The experience taught her early lessons in empathy, communication, and the power of listening, which helped her navigate and thrive in the corporate world.

Her job entailed going from house to house, convincing people to fill out questionnaires. One day, she was in the poorest areas; the next, she was at the vast houses of the wealthy. Initially, her team leader thought a convent-educated, fluent English-speaking girl would get a better response from the well-off, but she soon discovered they were likelier to set their dogs on her. Instead, she was accepted more at the lower-income groups. They loved chatting with her, and she gained insights into a different side of life, which helped her access the wealthy gentry and aided her career later.

After the field study, she was put in the research section, analyzing the data. She began to understand the research behind product launches and tracking market share. Those early days gave her critical insights into human behavior and sharpened her communication skills. More importantly, it taught her that being respectful and open-minded could break barriers across social classes.

Breaking Into Sales: The First Barrier

Sonali's next step was even more unconventional—she joined a direct sales team for EPABX systems, becoming the only woman on the team. In the mid-80s, sales were not considered a 'respectable' profession for women. Yet, she tackled the role head-on, learning to navigate customer expectations and gender biases.

Office automation was an upcoming field, so initially, one had to sell the concept and the product. It was a tough job, and personal conveyance was unheard of, so one had to take a bus or auto-rickshaw to a central point and walk the rest. The general perception was that if women had to do something challenging, it would be in male-dominated fields like defense, police, or administrative services. Taking up a sales job meant breaking barriers, which was not the field women dreamed of making headway in.

However, Sonali sank her teeth into the role and tried to do a good job. It was challenging and often thankless but interspersed with bright bits and lots of learning. Fortunately, her immediate boss was intuitive and unbiased, teaching her to handle the ropes. He also taught her the importance of understanding the systems beyond the job description, so her journey of going the extra mile started there. Soon, she hopped to another company and sold EPABXs. Though she didn't ultimately enjoy sales, the experience was formative, introducing her to workplace power-play and helping her develop resilience.

Finding Her Calling: A Career That Spanned Three Decades

Realizing her interest in broader aspects of marketing, she pursued a PGDM and eventually found her long-term professional home with Bry-Air, a Pahwa Group company headquartered in Delhi-NCR. The group was into products like dehumidifiers and other environment control equipment. That was the beginning of a long and fulfilling stint with its share of tears, frustration, and sheer exhaustion.

Sonali stayed with her next job for over 33 years, rising from Manager—Advertising and Publicity to Vice President—Corporate Affairs & HR. Her non-engineering background became her strength—she approached every challenge with a learning mindset and embraced responsibilities beyond her formal job description. Her ability to take on diverse responsibilities set her apart in a niche engineering company where technical expertise was prized.

She was often deputed to develop the market where the company opened new frontiers. Her first international stint was in Malaysia in the early 90s, followed by almost a year-long stint in Shanghai. It was a roller coaster and energizing, even when she was exhausted. She gained hands-on exposure to marketing and human resource development across various geographies, particularly Southeast Asia, China, the USA, and India.

Each additional responsibility opened new vistas for her. She became a member of the Management Committee groupwide. Apart from general management, her primary responsibility was overseeing marketing, corporate HR, branding strategy, and spearheading internal and external initiatives, including CSR. She also wore multiple additional hats during that time, apart from her core role.

During her career at Bry-Air, Sonali held positions with industry associations and NGOs. She served as National Chair of Advocacy for ISHRAE (Indian Society of Heating, Refrigeration,

Air-Conditioning Engineers), a member of the Board of Advisors for Literacy India (NGO), and a member of the women's security committee of Mash Virtual & Zammit India Pvt. Ltd. Each of these roles helped her grow.

Challenging Gender Norms and Self-Limiting Beliefs

Throughout her journey, Sonali challenged stereotypes—not just those imposed by society but the internal ones that limit individual growth. She believes the worst kind of discrimination is self-imposed and that competence and professionalism are the greatest equalizers. Whether navigating bias in the workplace or being the only woman in a male-dominated field, she built her credibility through performance, adaptability, and integrity.

Sonali faced implicit bias, whether expected to rely on male colleagues for technical explanations or underestimated because of her educational background. She understands that discrimination comes from many factors, and the worst is when you discriminate against yourself by putting yourself in a box as only a 'woman.'

There were several instances of discrimination; for example, in her first job, it was hinted that she did not have her degree from the 'right college.' But once she proved her competence, there would be grudging respect and eventual acceptance. She always worked towards being recognized and respected as a professional and did not look for any exceptional support or leeway because she was a woman.

Sonali's journey was also shaped by her experience as a single woman. She sees it as both a challenge and a blessing. Her parents provided a stable foundation and the freedom to forge her path. After their passing, she managed her home, career, and personal life alone—an experience that strengthened her independence and decision-making.

Her work brought her joy and balance. She believes that fulfillment comes from meaningful work, which has kept her through life's ups and downs.

Happily Unmarried: Freedom with Challenges

Being a single woman was both a challenge and a boon. Looking back, she was blessed with a solid foundation, with her parents giving her the liberty to carve her path while remaining supportive. After their deaths, she lived on her own and managed everything herself, which was not always easy. But her job, though challenging, was also exciting, and when you love your work, things work out well.

She learned to make her own decisions and stand by them, manage her finances, and do many things that a woman was typically not supposed to handle, including late-night work schedules.

Networking, Not Socializing

Sonali started as more of an introvert but grew into a skilled networker. She learned to hold her own at gatherings, understanding that networking involves developing rapport through continuous communication. She believes networking doesn't mean having many followers or greeting everyone in the database but developing rapport with continuous communication.

Over the years, she honed her skills and learned the importance of strategic networking. She defines networking not by the number of contacts but by the quality of connection and communication. Her ability to adapt to different settings—from boardrooms to industry forums—helped her thrive.

The Core Beliefs That Shaped Her Journey

When asked about the secret to her success, Sonali keeps it simple: adaptability, hard work, and the courage to take up responsibilities beyond her comfort zone. She has always focused on what can be done rather than why it can't. Her advice to women today is to step out of their comfort zones, stay informed, communicate well, be empathetic, and never stop growing. Reinvention is not a one-time act—it's a way of living.

For Sonali, what worked was her ability to take up varied responsibilities and adapt. There are no shortcuts. She made the best of all opportunities that came her way; even if there were none, she excelled. If she looks back today, her foundation years probably gave her the strength, resilience, discipline, freedom of thought process, and the ability to get along with everyone while maintaining her individuality.

She also learned to take ownership of her decisions and live by them, correcting course whenever necessary. Today, women have many opportunities. Her advice: step beyond your comfort zone, keep learning, lead with empathy, and let clear communication and knowledge light your path.

Shared with the permission of Sonali Dutta

Self-awareness & Empowerment

Stories for Self-awareness:

Self-awareness entails the process of introspection and comprehending oneself.

Here are some common experiences of many:

- *I tend to become angry when my work is criticized.*
- *I struggle to conceal my emotions. When I am upset, I often express my feelings openly, regardless of the context, which can occasionally result in losing clients.*
- *I have zero tolerance for subpar performance. I feel compelled to respond directly, irrespective of an individual's position within the company.*
- *I experience jealousy towards X.*
- *I feel anger towards Y.*
- *I feel content when this "____" occurs and dissatisfied when this "_____" takes place.*
- *And so on.*

One must gain a better understanding of oneself. Recognizing the reaction patterns, one tends to fall into is vital. One must be able to resist the instinct to react impulsively and navigate situations with finesse.

Achieving this is challenging. Several strategies must be employed simultaneously to cultivate this skill over time.

Stories for Empowerment

In all the case studies, without exception, everyone emphasized the need for continuous learning, lifetime learning and domain expertise, to be on top of the subject matter. In addition, we can notice that Subhadra, Nemi, Smita, Gayatri and Nayeema are able to contribute to larger society and make an impact to the society.

Self-awareness and Empowerment: A Journey through Maslow's Hierarchy

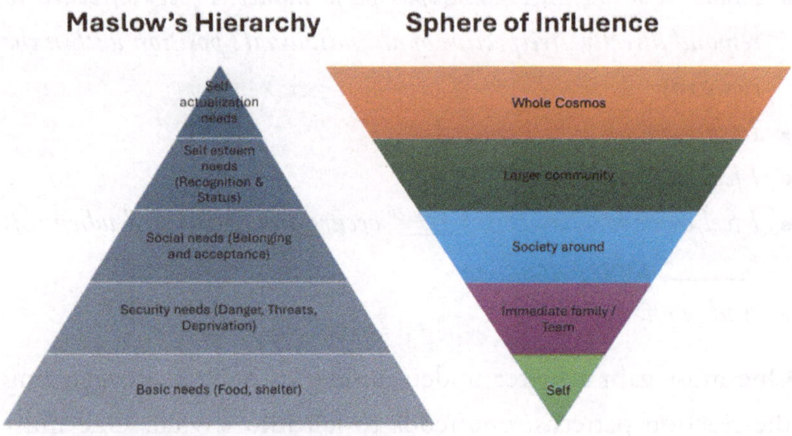

Self-awareness and empowering yourself are not just ways to move up in your job; they are also ways to move towards fulfilment and having a more meaningful life. Let us examine through the lens of **Maslow's Hierarchy of Needs**, they go beyond the pursuit of top jobs and material success. They lead us to the ultimate goal of self-actualization, which means reaching our fullest potential. This section talks about how being self-aware and giving ourselves power can help us on our journey, from learning basic job skills to reaching higher intellectual and spiritual levels of happiness.

Level 1: The Foundation: Getting ahead in your career to meet basic needs

Maslow's pyramid starts with **physiological and safety needs**, which are the most basic needs for staying alive and being stable. At this stage, as depicted in 'Sphere of Influence' pyramid, one is focused only on self and survival. In terms of a work, this means getting a job, making money, and feeling safe. When we first start working, we focus on building **foundation skills** that will make us efficient, reliable, and productive. To meet basic needs and build a strong base for growth, you need to have these skills.

For example, being good at **managing our time**, **communicating clearly,** and **being aware of our emotions** not only makes us better workers, but it also helps teams trust each other and work together. These skills are essential for a good career because they help us meet our basic needs and set us up for bigger goals.

Level 2: The Middle Layers: Belonging, Esteem, and Empowerment are the middle layers.

As we get better at our jobs, we move up Maslow's hierarchy to the levels of belongingness, love and esteem. In this case, the focus shifts from oneself to making a circle of influence (friends and getting noticed). This is where **empowerment** is very important. At this stage, as depicted in the 'Sphere of Influence' pyramid, the circle of influence keeps growing: on the family side, the family increases, and on the career side, teams come under your control.

To be empowered, we must first be self-aware, i.e. our own skills and abilities, weaknesses, and emotional triggers. It also means using this awareness to take charge of our lives, make smart choices, and motivate other people. For example, a self-aware leader can handle the dynamics of the workplace with understanding and clarity, helping their team feel like they belong there. They create a place where everyone feels valued and accepted, they advocate for inclusive policies and help others grow by mentoring.

It is important to **keep training and developing your skills and abilities** at this stage. Certain percentage of our income should be allocated for continuous learning. Spending in training programs, requesting for feedback, and taking on challenging new tasks not only help our careers but also make us feel better about our own self-worth. As we get older, we start to see ourselves as strong and capable, able to bring about change and make a difference.

Level 3: Self-actualization and the Ultimate Purpose are at the pinnacle.

At the top of Maslow's scale is **self-actualization**, which means reaching our full potential. At this point, the goal of job success goes beyond material gains and turns into a search for meaning, purpose, and fulfillment. Self-actualization isn't about getting to the top of the company; it's about becoming the best version of ourselves and making a difference in the world for the better. At this stage, as depicted in the 'Sphere of Influence' pyramid, the circle of influence becomes larger: more responsibilities and larger teams, and socially also, bigger communities, come into contact with you.

To reach self-actualization, we need to grow in all dimensions of our lives: **physical, mental, emotional, intellectual and spiritual**. This all-around method fits with Maslow's idea of transcendence, which means going beyond our own success to motivate and inspire others. For instance, a leader who has reached self-actualization doesn't just focus on the goals of the organization; they also want to leave a legacy of empowering and including everyone.

Self-Awareness and Empowerment Guide with Useful Insights

1. Self-awareness:

Overview:

Evaluate your skills, interests, values, and personality traits to understand Your personality type and which path to be taken.

Self assessment Actions for personality assessment

- Take personality and career assessment tests (e.g., Myers-Briggs, Holland Code).
  - https://www.themyersbriggs.com/en-US/Products-and-Services/Myers-Briggs
  - https://www.roguecc.edu/counseling/hollandcodes/about.asp
  - https://johari-window.com/
- Reflect on your past experiences, strengths, and areas for improvement.
- Identify your core values and what you seek in a career (e.g., work-life balance, creativity).

360 degree feedback

- This tool allows taking feedback from all around – higher levels, peers, employees reporting to you, customers etc. This give the perspectives of all the people working with you, gives very insightful feedback for self awareness.

Journaling

- Every day end, spending 15mins reflecting how the day has gone by – this gives a chance for honest introspection of our behaviour throughout the day and understanding emotions.

Meditation

Emotional Intelligence assessment

All these tools help one to get valuable insights into their own behaviors, motivations, and relationships; understanding their own Strengths, and areas of improvement; and thereby, ability to respond to situations and not react.

2. Empowerment:

Empowerment is getting trained upkeeping your skills in personal and professional areas continuously. Empowerment is the best way that one can reach their full potential.

Skill gap filling: It is vital to enhance job-related abilities and keep updated knowledge in the field. Allocate a certain percentage of your income towards self-educational pursuits (both subject-specific and personal growth).

- In the early career days, building basic skills, confidence and dependability, like being efficient, honest, and emotionally aware.
- As you move up in your job, empowerment changes into leadership, which requires emotional intelligence, strategic insight, and the ability to motivate others.

Empowerment is based on a desire to keep learning, be flexible, and accept changes (being adaptable) in a world that is changing quickly. It builds a mindset of resilience, self-belief, and constant improvement, which gives people the tools they need to not only deal with problems but also do well in their jobs. It's not a goal to become empowered; it's a journey of growth, leadership, and a never-ending search for greatness.

3. Embrace a Growth Mindset:

Accept that problems are chances to learn and improve; this is called a growth mindset. If you want to reach higher goals, think about your failures.

4. Lead with purpose:

Always be an example for others as you grow. Speaking or writing about your experiences, problems, and successes can inspire and motivate people around you, and this can also be published on social media. For instance, speaking openly about how you overcame an interpersonal problem in your job can give others hope and direction.

5. Aim for holistic growth:

Work on improving your physical, mental, social, and spiritual well-being each day. Any one of these aspects cannot be neglected.

6. Contribute something Greater:

Focus less on your success and more on making a big difference in the lives of others and society as a whole. Try to find ways to give back to society. and leave a legacy of empowerment, whether it's through mentoring, advocating, or community work.

Self-actualization, Self-Awareness, and Empowerment All Come Together

To reach self-actualization, you need to be self-aware and give yourself power. If you know more about yourself, you can take charge of your life and make choices that align with your goals and purpose. We must be empowered to use what you've learned to make fundamental changes, motivate others, and leave a heritage of growth and acceptance.

In the end, moving up in your career to become your best self

To reach self-actualization, one must not follow a straight line. Instead, one must constantly learn, grow, and change. We must become more self-aware and accept our power to get through this journey with focus, purpose, and strength. We not only help others succeed in their personal and professional lives, but we also inspire and encourage them along the way.

In the end, genuine happiness comes from finding a balance between knowing yourself and being able to make a difference in the world. Once we reach self-actualization, we stop trying to get the best jobs and make the most money. Instead, we focus on a higher mission that improves our lives and leaves a legacy of growth, acceptance, and empowerment. **"What a man can be, he must be,"** said Maslow. For the sake of all people, let's all try to be the best versions of ourselves.

Exercises

Exercises for confidence, self-reflection, and continuous learning in building a fulfilling career.

Exercise 1: The "Confidence Journal"

- **Step 1:** Every day, write down one thing you accomplished, no matter how small. For example: "I handled a difficult client conversation with ease."
- **Step 2:** Reflect on what skills or qualities helped you succeed in that moment (e.g., "I stayed calm under pressure").
- **Step 3:** Identify one area where you'd like to grow (e.g., public speaking, technical skills). Research resources (books, courses, mentors) to help you improve.

Exercise 2: Conduct a **Quarterly Career Review**. Every three months, ask yourself:

- What have I achieved?
- What challenges did I face, and how did I overcome them?
- What do I want to focus on in the next quarter?
- Expand your "Confidence Journal" to include "Lessons Learned" from challenges or failures. For example:

- o "I didn't get the promotion, but I learned that I need to improve my public speaking skills." This shifts your mindset from self-criticism to growth.

Additional Idea:

- The "Future Self" Visualization: Spend 10 minutes visualizing where you want to be in 5 years. Write a letter from your future self to your current self, offering advice and encouragement. This exercise helps you clarify your goals and build motivation.

Reader's Feedback

- Which story from the above stories is closer to your own situation?
- Do you have any additional ideas for demonstrating Self Awareness and Empowerment?

CHAPTER 7

CONCLUSION

The Integrated Path to Growth and Fulfillment

Life is a mosaic of different events, difficulties, and chances. Every part of the puzzle—negotiating for what you deserve, getting past systemic barriers, balancing work and life, or becoming more self-aware—adds to the bigger picture of a happy and powerful life.

Career Progression Guidance: Lessons from Inspiring Journeys

The stories of myself, Dr. Ambuja Udas, Jane, Abha, Vidyarthi, Srinivasa Prasad, Sonali Dutta, Sunil Khurana, Nemichandra, Meera, Ravi, Dr. Subhadra, Law. Smita, Dr. Gayatri, and ICWA Nayeema Kouser offer a wealth of insights into navigating the complexities of career progression. These narratives, spanning diverse industries and roles, reveal common themes and strategies that can guide anyone seeking to advance in their professional journey. Here, we distill these lessons into a cohesive framework for career progression, emphasizing resilience, adaptability, and self-awareness.

1. **Embrace Lifelong Learning and Adaptability**
2. **Build a Strong Professional Network**
3. **Be Assertive and Advocate for Yourself**
4. **Overcome Systemic Barriers with Resilience**
5. **Strive for Work-Life Integration, Not Just Balance**
6. **Develop Self-Awareness and Empowerment**
7. **Take Calculated Risks and Embrace Challenges**
8. **Focus on Impact and Results**
9. **Be a Role Model and Pay It Forward**
10. **Stay True to Your Values and Purpose**

Conclusion

Career progression is not a linear path but a journey filled with challenges, opportunities, and moments of growth. The stories of these remarkable individuals remind us that success is not just about reaching the top—it's about the resilience, adaptability, and self-awareness you develop along the way. By embracing lifelong learning, building strong networks, advocating for yourself, and staying true to your values, you can navigate the complexities of your career and achieve both professional fulfillment and personal satisfaction. Remember, your journey is unique—own it, learn from it, and let it inspire others.

To further strengthen these ideas, here is story of a historical figure who demonstrated all these qualities and continues to inspire everyone even today.

Ahilya Bai Holkar: A Story of Resilience and Empowerment

Systemic barriers

Ahilya Bai was born in 1725 in a village by name Chondi, Maharashtra. She was born into a simple and humble family. But the then Subedar finds a spark in this young girl and gets her home as his daughter-in-law. In those days when women were relegated to domestic chores, she was mentored by her father-in-law, who encouraged her into education, war-fare, finance, and different aspects of running the government. She faced severe systemic barriers in a patriarchial society but fought through all of those.

Networking & Mentoring

After her husband's death, Ahilya faced many challenges. The political landscape was full of men who did not agree on a woman as a leader. However, she worked hard to build a network of allies, nobles, and military leaders from neighboring districts. She created a formidable force with the help of these allies and protected her provenance.

She surrounded herself with wise advisors who gave her right inputs from time to time. Mentoring by her father-in-law and continuous support from these wise people around her helped her gain the respect of her peers and establish her authority as a leader.

Negotiation & Assertiveness

She ascended the throne of Indore in 1767. After this, she handled the conflicts with rival states and negotiated treaties in favor of her kingdom using excellent negotiation skills and assertiveness. She made bold decisions by making women to earn money by weaving saris, huge reforms in administration and taxation, and improving the welfare of all citizens of her kingdom. With her diplomatic prowess, she tied up with neighboring rulers and created alliances to strengthen her kingdom's safety and prosperity.

Work-Life Balance

As a queen, Ahilya had to balance her family as a mother of two children along with her responsibilities of running her territory. She used to spare time for her children by delegating responsibilities to her trusted staff. She prioritized family and community. The whole kingdom used to refer to her as mother. She had many initiatives for women's welfare, included them in various activities and promoted their well-being.

Self-Actualization and Empowerment

Her period as a queen is well known for the emphasis on social justice and empowerment. She worked towards holistic development of her kingdom, invested in infrastructure, education, and health care. She made sure that everybody had access to resources and opportunities, including marginalised communities. Her journey of self-actualization was demonstrated by transcending the then social norms and beliefs. She symbolises of strength and resilience, inspiring generations to come to take leadership roles and become holistic leaders.

This case study is a testament of leader who empowered her people and championed social justice. Her story reflects the impact a visionary leader can create in shaping a better society.

Conclusion: The Journey Beyond the Book

As we come to the end of this book, remember that growth is not a destination but a journey. The principles given here, networking, negotiation, overcoming barriers, work-life balance, and self-awareness, are not just tools for achieving career progression; they are pathways to a more fulfilling and empowered life. Embrace the challenges, celebrate the victories, and strive to become the best version of yourself.

In the words of Lao Tzu, *"The journey of a thousand miles begins with a single step."* [5] Take that step today. Reflect on your values, set your priorities, and take deliberate action toward your goals. And as you grow, remember to lift others along the way. True fulfillment lies in achieving success and creating a legacy of growth, inclusivity, and empowerment.

Exercise integrates all areas

Using 7 step career framework, develop Career Plan for yourself:

1. Self-Awareness

Using the different tools given in the previous section, get valuable insights into their behaviors, motivations, and relationships. Arrive at the SWOT matrix.

2. Set Career Goals

Overview:

Define clear, achievable career goals based on your self-assessment.

Actions:

- Use the SMART criteria (Specific, Measurable, Achievable, Relevant, Time-bound) to set your goals.
- Consider both short-term (1-2 years) and long-term (3-5 years) goals.
- Write down your goals to create accountability.

3. Research Career Options

Overview:

Explore various career options: Internally – With the same department or other departments; Externally – search in LinkedIn and others

Actions:

- Investigate the roles that match your skills and aspirations.
- Conduct information gathering exercise to study the opportunity thoroughly.
- Utilize online resources to learn about job.

4. In parallel, work on developing Skills, Qualifications and competencies

Overview:

Identify and acquire the skills and qualifications necessary for your chosen career path.

Actions:

- Pursue relevant trainings and certifications.
- Gain practical experience through doing projects
- Attend different forums and events to get a wider perspective on the subject.

5. Build / use Network and Mentorship

- Explained in the chapter on this subject above

6. Create a Personal Brand

- Explained in that section above

7. Evaluate and Adjust Your Career Plan

Overview:

Regularly assess your progress and make adjustments to your career plan as needed.

Actions:

- Set aside time periodically (e.g., quarterly or annually) to review your goals and achievements.
- Seek feedback from mentors or peers to gain insights into your performance and areas for improvement.
- Be flexible and willing to adapt your goals and strategies based on changes in your interests or the job market.

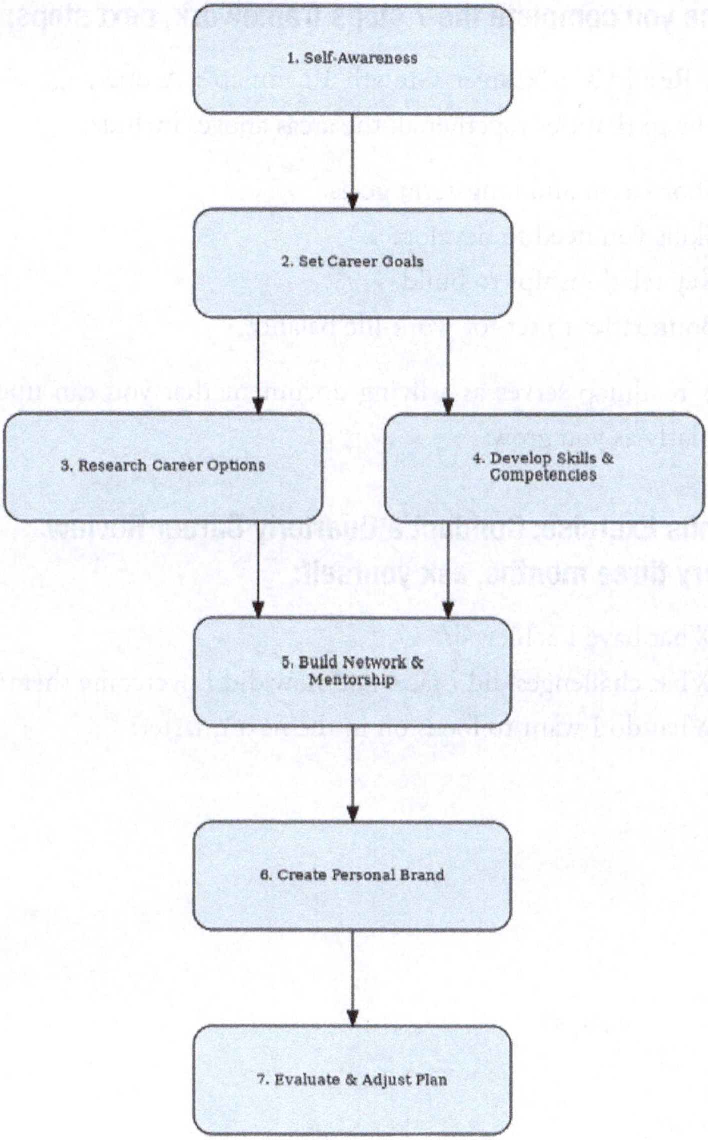

Figure: 7 Step Framework

Once you complete the 7 steps framework, next steps:

The Result is a "Career Growth Roadmap": A one-page visual roadmap that ties together all the areas above. Include:

- Short-term and long-term goals.
- Skills you need to develop.
- Key relationships to build.
- Boundaries to set for work-life balance.

This roadmap serves as a living document that you can update regularly as you grow.

Bonus Exercise: Conduct a Quarterly Career Review. Every three months, ask yourself:

- What have I achieved?
- What challenges did I face, and how did I overcome them?
- What do I want to focus on in the next quarter?

APPENDIX – BACKGROUND & DATA

Significant challenges in career progression

Reaching the highest levels of management is a highly sought-after objective for many professionals at mid- and senior levels.

Consistent performance evaluations may include phrases like: "You still have room for improvement."; "You need to adopt a more strategic mindset."; "You are overly empathetic and lack the necessary detachment."

With such persistent critiques, individuals may experience imposter syndrome and develop self-doubt. It is important to resist being adversely affected by outside negativity that could compromise one's professional achievements.

This phenomenon leads to **Career stagnation** and individuals remain stuck in middle management for extended periods. Regardless of their efforts and achievements, they often face no promotions or salary increases. Reduced salaries compared to their peers, which is a direct financial loss, **Pay disparity**. **Depression and demotivation** as an individual's self-confidence gets smashed out and imposter syndrome will set in.

The Organization also gets impacted badly as, by sidelining the deserving candidate, a performing individual would lose motivation and it also demotivates others who are watching this performing individual.

As one ascends the corporate ladder, the number of available positions diminishes, and **fierce competition** will occur. Competing against equally qualified colleagues can be intimidating.

Skill deficiency is another challenge. Top management roles demand a wider range of skills, including a grasp of the latest technology developments and solutions using these, the ability to negotiate and commit and deliver to commitments, strategic thinking, stakeholder engagement, and emotional intelligence, which may not have been fully cultivated in earlier positions.

The demands of higher performance can cause one to lose focus on **work-life balance** and be focused on work all the time. This often leads to burnout, which negatively affects personal health and job effectiveness.

Perceptions and biases are natural phenomena that arise due to an individual's style, age, gender, experience, and other factors. They come into play automatically and can cause obstacles to advancement. Some may be conscious biases, and some may be unconscious biases.

The fast pace of technological and organizational transformations necessitates continual upskilling and the ability to adapt. **Adaptability to change** is another challenge from the individual's side.

Gender Bias Impact on Women & Data

The "Glass ceiling" refers to the invisible barriers (the glass) that women and minorities can see through to elite roles yet cannot attain (the ceiling) despite their qualifications and accomplishments. Marilyn Loden introduced this phrase in a speech in 1978.

Here are some key statistics highlighting systemic obstacles for women in the corporate arena.

Gender Pay gap is a prominent phenomenon worldwide. As the World Economic Forum reported in 2023, women worldwide earn approximately 60-75% of what men make for similar positions. In the United States, the pay gap is around 83%, meaning women earn $0.83 for each dollar men earn.

Women in Leadership roles is a known problem area. A 2022 report from McKinsey & Company revealed that women only occupy 28% of senior vice president positions and 23% of C-suite roles in the U.S. corporate landscape. The same report also highlighted that women of color are even less represented.

The McKinsey report noted that women are less promoted to managerial roles than their male counterparts (by 16%), contributing to the leadership disparity.

A 2020 survey conducted by LeanIn.Org found that 50% of women experienced some form of gender bias in their workplaces, including having their ideas dismissed or being interrupted. This **workplace discrimination** is common in most places.

Family Leave policy: According to the Society for Human Resource Management (SHRM), just 23% of U.S. companies provide paid parental leave, disproportionately affecting women who often assume primary caregiving responsibilities.

The National Women's Law Center reported that 60% of women with children under 18 are employed, yet many encounter difficulties due to the steep cost of childcare, which can exceed $1,000 monthly in specific locations. **Childcare challenges** are high for women. A 2021 report by McKinsey highlighted that women in the U.S. still undertake approximately 75% of household chores and child-rearing responsibilities, resulting in increased stress and reduced satisfaction with **work-life balance** for women.

Women drop out of their careers or experience interruptions in child care and family responsibilities. At the same time, men don't face such pressure due to patriarchal thinking patterns.

A report from McKinsey noted that during the COVID-19 pandemic, women were more likely to face difficulties with remote work, especially in households where caregiving duties were not equally shared. Many women, particularly mothers, reported feeling overwhelmed by the dual demands of home and work.

A study by the Kaiser Family Foundation found that women are more likely than men to report unaddressed **healthcare needs**, especially regarding reproductive health services. Findings from a 2020 Deloitte Global Survey indicated that women are more susceptible to stress tied to work-life balance. About 60% of women reported stress or burnout at work, compared to 45% of men.

A study from McKinsey in 2020 emphasized that **women in leadership positions** often experience **heightened stress**, mainly due to gender roles and the increased demands of their jobs.

Gender-based violence is not uncommon. A survey by the Equal Employment Opportunity Commission (EEOC)[6] revealed that almost indicated that nearly 1 in 3 women reported experiencing sexual harassment in the workplace.[7]

Legal barriers for women and policy changes required are immense.

These statistics illustrate the systemic barriers women face in the corporate world and underscore the need for empowering women in the workplace.

REFERENCES

[1] (2016). Saskatoon By. https://ecommons.usask.ca/bitstream/handle/10388/ETD-2011-08-63/CERVANTES-THESIS.pdf%3Bjsessionid%3DB708896602C05056E32953BCF51D1B94?sequence%3D4

[2] HBR – change exchang.studio. https://changeexchange.studio/archives/tag/hbr

[3] Taking out the Trash. http://forum.animalpak.com/showthread.php?31309-Taking-out-the-Trash

[4] Eisenhower Matrix: Career and family: Finding the right balance - Noustro. https://noustro.com/soft-skills/career-and-family-finding-the-right-balance/

[5] The Journey of a Thousand Miles Begins With a Single Step Quotes - Motivation and Love. https://motivationandlove.com/the-journey-of-a-thousand-miles-begins-with-a-single-step-quotes

[6] Kill the Imposter: How Imposter Syndrome Affects Black Women in the Workplace – Gender and Intersectional Analysis. https://sites.tufts.edu/gender/kill-the-imposter-how-imposter-syndrome-affects-black-women-in-the-workplace/

[7] Types of sexual harassment in a Florida workplace | Law Office of William M Julien PA. https://www.attorneyjulien.com/blog/2017/10/types-of-sexual-harassment-in-a-florida-workplace/

Here are the top 10 references for understanding and exploring the concept of a growth mindset.

Books

1. **Mindset: The New Psychology of Success** by Carol S. Dweck
2. **Grit: The Power of Passion and Perseverance** by Angela Duckworth
3. **The Power of Yet** by Carol S. Dweck (Children's Book)
4. **Mindset: The New Psychology of Success** by Carol S. Dweck
5. **Peak: Secrets from the New Science of Expertise** by Anders Ericsson and Robert Pool

Articles and Papers

6. **"The Role of Mindsets in Learning and Achievement"** by Carol S. Dweck
7. **"Mindsets and the Motivation to Learn"** by Dweck, C. S. & Leggett, E. L.

Online Resources

8. **Growth Mindset: A Guide for Educators** (Edutopia)
9. **Mindset Works**
10. **TED Talk: "The Power of Believing That You Can Improve" by Carol S. Dweck**

These references offer a comprehensive overview of the growth mindset concept, its implications, and practical applications in various contexts.

Readers Feedback

Leadership in Action – We'd Love Your Feedback! Your insights help us grow the conversation around intentional, inclusive leadership.

Scan the QR code to share your thoughts

Or, fill the form:

https://forms.gle/HCYesXrv3gTVj7rUA

Or, email to padmackr@gmail.com